ANYTHING
YOU CAN DO
I CAN DO
BETTER

ANYTHING
YOU CAN DO
I CAN DO
BETTER

A GIRL'S GUIDE TO GUY STUFF

by Leigh Phillips & Jennifer Axen

CHRONICLE BOOKS
SAN FRANCISCO

Library of Congress Cataloging-in-Publication Data available.

ISBN-10: 0-8118-5396-9
ISBN-13: 978-0-8118-5396-5

Manufactured in Canada

Cover and book designed by Yoshie Matsumoto

Distributed in Canada by Raincoast Books
9050 Shaughnessy Street
Vancouver, British Columbia V6P 6E5

10 9 8 7 6 5 4 3 2 1

Chronicle Books LLC
85 Second Street
San Francisco, California 94105

www.chroniclebooks.com

To our dads, Kelvin Phillips and Curt Axen,
who taught us to be "can do" women.

Contents

Contents

I Can ... Read This Book!

Have you ever wanted to sit in a bar and talk about sports with total strangers? Have you ever felt baffled by the complexities of the March Madness office pool? Have you ever fantasized about being a pool shark? For all the women of the world who are sick and tired of being laughed at, intimidated, and just plain excluded by the guys, help is finally at hand!

We have developed a comprehensive how-to manual for any girl looking to play with the boys—and beat them at their own game. Despite the huge strides made toward equality over the last one hundred years, a few bastions of male prowess remain. *Anything You Can Do I Can Do Better* breaks through these final barriers and enables all women to stand at the watercooler and gab with assurance, even during play-off season.

Within these six chapters, we provide quick and easy instructions for mastering a wide range of guy-centric topics—everything from the rules of Fantasy Football to packing a car trunk, from carving meat to fitting a sofa through a door. Each topic is concisely covered (let's face it—their stuff really isn't that complicated!) and includes little cheat boxes to help you learn the buzz words for each skill and dazzle friends with your newfound knowledge. To help you make these skills your own, we've added some advice about how to give all this guy stuff a much-needed feminine twist.

Whether you want to bust some heads in the boardroom, win a spitting contest, or puff on a cigar while sipping whiskey, this book virtually guarantees your success. In no time, you will confidently stride where few women have gone before, and you'll look fabulous while doing it!

Our aim is to demystify some of the masculine arts so that their secret world will no longer be quite so secret. We see no reason why the guys get to barbecue while the girls have to do the dishes! We see no reason why our male colleagues exclude us on trips to the golf course! We see no reason why they get to kill insects while we get to go shopping! Okay, maybe that last one is pretty reasonable, but you get the point.

Within these pages you'll find everything you ever wanted to know about the world of men. Once you reach the end of this book you are sure to agree with us—anything they can do, we really *can* do better!

chapter 1

Game Time

If you're anything like most women, you've experienced a situation like the following: You are hanging out with a group of friends when the subject turns to the sport du jour—basketball, hockey, or football, perhaps. Just a moment ago, you were in the swing of things, making conversation and tossing out clever quips. Now the topic being discussed is the infield-fly rule, and you are suddenly sidelined. Sure, you'd like to talk March Madness or join in on the Fantasy Football pool at the office. The problem is, you just don't know enough to keep up. When it comes to talking about Division 1 Teams, Texas Hold 'Em, and draft picks, you suffer from underexposure. Fear not; help is on the way.

It's no revelation that many girls grow up with very little exposure to and guidance in sports. The causes for this are manifold: lack of programs, scant mentoring, and few role models. You may have an aunt who is really into baseball or a friend who likes to go to soccer games, but—let's face it—these women are in the minority.

According to theories of evolutionary biology, the human brain only stores the knowledge deemed to be important to that individual's life. Think of the brain as similar to flypaper: Information is everywhere, and it races by us all the time, but the only thing that sticks is what is important in our personal world. Historically speaking, for women, sports usually just don't make the cut. But that's about to change.

You have what it takes to get in the game; you just need a little practice if you want to learn how to arm wrestle, make a mint at the track, or just sound like you know what's going on in the sports world.

I Can . . . Win March Madness!

Not to be confused with *spring fever*, March Madness is the name given to the National Collegiate Athletic Association (NCAA) Men's and Women's Basketball tournament. It is, however, not just a sporting frenzy; it is also one of the most-bet-upon sporting events of the year, with an incredible $2.5 billion wagered in office pools and on Internet sites across the country. There are two things you need to understand about March Madness: the tournament itself and, more important, the office pool.

The Tournament

March Madness generally focuses on Division I of the men's basketball tournament. Of the 327 teams in Division I, only 65, chosen by a selection committee, are invited to the tournament.

These 65 teams are categorized according to four geographical regions: East, South, Midwest, and West. Each region starts with 16 teams, each of which is assigned a seed number, the best team being awarded the number 1 seed and the worst team the number 16 seed. Because 65 is an odd number, one region begins with 17 teams and the two lowest-ranked teams in that region play for the number 16 seed. Most often, one of the higher-seeded teams will win the tournament.

The beginning of the tournament moves pretty quickly, with the number of teams paring down from 65 to the "Sweet Sixteen" within the first four days. Those remaining 16 will battle through the rest of March, and the surviving teams from each region (the "Final Four") play for the championship in early April. The semifinal games are played on the first Saturday in April, and the winners face off for the title on the following Monday.

The Office Pool ....

There is undoubtedly someone in your office who coordinates the pool every year. He will most likely identify himself by babbling endlessly about "the brackets" and will be more than happy to take your money. (Be warned: Gambling is still illegal and you may want to check company policy before ponying up your stake.) Each member of the pool contributes the same set dollar amount. The winner of the pool takes home the cash. Sounds simple, right?

Each pool has its own rules, but the most common March Madness pool runs on a points system, with points awarded to pool participants for each correctly predicted game. Some pools are simple, offering the same number of points for each win, but in others the points

increase as the teams progess toward the end of the tournament. For example:

Round One: 3 points per game

Round Two: 5 points per game

Sweet Sixteen: 11 points per game

Elite Eight: 17 points per game

Final Four: 30 points per game

Championship: 40 points

To win the pool, you must predict the winners of as many games as possible to have the highest point total.

Your picks are made prior to the beginning of the tournament and cannot be changed. You will try to predict the winner of every game, starting with the regionals. Your predicted winner of each regional will (we hope) be one of the Final Four. Then it is just a matter of picking the championship team for the big win. The further your picks advance, the more points you earn. If you lose all of your initial games, you basically suck, and you and your loser teams are out of the game and you lose the money you initially put down. In the case of a tie (if two people earn the same number of points in the pool), you may also have to predict the total number of points scored in the final championship game. In this situation, the person who most accurately predicts the points scored in the final game wins.

Making Your Picks ··············

Start from the final game and work backward. This means picking your championship team first, and then, obviously, marking them to win in every game they play before that. The real points come in accurately predicting the Final Four. For this you might need to do a little homework. Most often it will be four of the highest-seeded teams that make it to this stage—but not always. The *upset teams* are part of what puts the "madness" into March Madness. Do a little research on the track record of the highest-seeded teams (how they performed on the road, their conference record, and so on). You'll be able to find plenty of Web sites that list all of this information, saving you lots of work. Pick your championship team, two high-seeded teams, and

then perhaps a lower-seeded team (but not a 15 or 16 seed) to make up your Final Four.

Here's a tip: Find a team that may not be high on the list but happens to have one outstanding, superstar player. A team with one major star and solid, experienced support players could make it to the Final Four. Have fun with your picks, but be sensible; a number 16 seed is unlikely to beat a number 1 seed. If all else fails, base your picks on who has the best uniforms or the weirdest school mascot. You just might win, because, for some bizarre reason, people who know nothing about basketball always seem to win the office pool and walk off with the cash.

GIRL'S WORLD

Let's not forget that the women's NCAA basketball teams are also playing in their annual tournament. Start an office pool for the ladies' teams and help spark more interest in women's athletics.

I Can... Explain the Infield-Fly Rule!

In every sport there exists one key rule that, if you understand it and can explain it, proves your true knowledge of, and dedication to, the game. For baseball fans, that rule is the infield-fly rule.

The Rule

In a nutshell, the infield-fly rule was created to prevent an easy double play for the pitching side if the batter hits a pop-up on the infield and there are runners on the bases. At some point in the history of baseball, an infielder realized that if he let the ball drop on purpose he could then quickly pick it up, potentially throwing two players out instead of catching one. But that would be unfair. Hence, the infield-fly rule was established. So now, if a batter hits an infield fly, the umpire will shout, "Infield fly; batter is out," or he will simply point to the sky. The batter is retired and play continues.

How the Rule Is Applied

That all sounds reasonably straight-forward, right? Not so fast. Let us not forget that this is the world of sports and, as is the case with many sports-related rules, confusion can arise in the details and the circumstances under which the rule is applied. Knowing when the rule can and cannot be called is as important as simply knowing what it means.

The infield-fly rule is a judgment call on the part of the umpire—the umpire must believe that the ball can be caught with "reasonable effort." The rule can only be applied when there are fewer than two outs (if there are already two outs you would only need one out to end the inning and the possibility of a double play would be moot). Runners must be on first and second, or the bases must be loaded. Just one runner on first is not enough, because by the time the infielder let the ball drop and threw to second to get the runner out, the batter would already be at first base so you still only get one out instead of two. Once the infield fly is called, the runners do not have to advance even if the ball is not caught. However, they can choose to do so at their own risk, as they would with a pop-up.

Another source of confusion is whether or not the call can be made for both fair and foul balls. The rule can only be called if the ball is fair. If the ball lands in or rolls into foul territory, then the batter is not out (he simply gets another chance at bat), even if the umpire has called the infield-fly rule. Use of the rule is always a judgment call on the part of the umpire, who must declare it while the ball is still in the air. For this reason, in certain cases the umpire may call, "Infield fly if fair," applying the rule only if the ball lands in fair territory.

You may have to read this more than once to fully grasp the intricacies of the rule. But once you do, your place as a true baseball fan cannot be denied.

The Jargon

Double play: A defensive play in which two offensive players are put out as a result of one action

Fly ball: A ball that goes high in the air when batted, also known as a "pop-up."

Force play: The runner already on base is forced to run in order to vacate the base for the next runner.

Random Fact: The infield-fly rule was established in 1920 to eliminate an unfair advantage to the pitching team.

I Can . . . Play Pool!

The pool table is surrounded by a group of biker guys, a haze of smoke hangs in the air, and a sexy woman in tight jeans sidles up to the table and throws down a $20 bill with her challenge. She then proceeds to school every guy in the room and walks out with a pocketful of cash. Let's admit it, ladies: we've all had that fantasy at one point in our lives, only to come face-to-face with the harsh reality that the best we can do is sink a ball without scratching. Well, we may not be able to train you to become pool sharks, but we can stave off any major humiliations.

Holding the Stick

The first step to mastering the game of pool is to learn how to hold the stick, or cue, properly. Your grip on the stick (with your back hand, the right hand for most people) should be loose, and your wrist should point straight downward. The other hand is used to form the bridge, which you use to support the stick while you take your shot. The type of bridge you choose depends on what feels most comfortable to you.

To form an open bridge, lay your hand flat on the table, raise your knuckles to form a peak in the center, bring your thumb forward so it touches your first finger, and then spread your remaining three fingers to firmly stabilize your hand on the table. The cue will rest on the crease between your thumb and first finger. Alternatively, keep your fist closed instead of spreading your fingers on the table.

For a closed bridge, make a fist and place it on the table, open your first finger and thumb, and then bring them together to form a circle that the cue will go through. Spread your remaining fingers on the table for support.

Your bridge is the cornerstone of your game. If it's too strong, too weak, too high, too low, too loose, or too anything, your shot will reflect this.

The Stroke ·

Before you take your shot, you'll need to work on your stroke. The following points are all key to a great stroke:

- Plant your feet far apart, with your bridge hand well in front of you. This forms the stable "triangle pose."

- Take practice strokes to loosen your arm and perfect your aim.

- Keep the stick parallel to the ground. One of the most common beginner's errors is to hold the stick at too much of an angle.

- Hold your head very low, with your chin almost on the stick.

- Keep your eye as close to the stick as possible in order to better visualize the aim of your shot.

The Shot ·

Now that you have your setup, it's time for the tricky part: aiming. Hitting one round object against another round object and trying to get them to go where you want is pretty difficult. The first step is to find the ideal point of contact on the object ball (the one you are trying to sink). The easiest way to figure out the best point of contact is to take your stick and pretend you are hitting the object ball directly, visualizing the path the ball must take in order to go into the pocket. That spot is where you need to aim your cue ball (the white ball). Next, set up your shot so that your cue ball will hit the point of contact on the object ball. Your shot should be firm, but not too hard.

The Game ·····················

Eight ball is the most commonly played pool game. Place one cue ball and fifteen numbered balls on the table, which are racked with the 8 ball (the solid black ball) in the center of the triangle. One player will aim to sink balls 1 through 7 (solid colors) and the other will try to sink balls 9 through 15 (stripes). Ball 8 (solid black) remains on the table until the very end. To start, the first player "breaks" by hitting the cue ball into the racked number balls (whether you are playing stripes or solids is determined by which type you sink first. Once you sink either a solid or a striped ball, you must hit only that group of balls for the rest of the game). Your turn continues until you fail to pocket a ball. Once you have pocketed your entire group of balls, you may try for the 8 ball. Whoever sinks the 8 ball first wins. If you accidentally sink the eight ball before finishing your group, or if you scratch (see "The Jargon") while trying to sink the 8 ball, you lose the game.

Practice really does make perfect, so now that you know the basics, you should head on down to your local pool hall and get started. Soon enough, that pool shark fantasy just might become a reality.

The Jargon

Cue ball: The white ball

To sink or **pocket:** To hit a numbered ball into a pocket

To scratch: To hit the cue ball into a pocket

Rack: The triangular frame used to set up the balls before the game begins

Becoming a true poker stud requires a mixture of skill, nerve, and cunning. A thorough grounding in the basics is essential, but to truly conquer the casino you need to hone your observational skills and perfect your poker face.

The Rules

Essentially there are two ways to win the pot: either have the highest-ranking hand, or fool everyone else into thinking you have the highest-ranking hand. Each player puts a predetermined amount of money into the pot before the cards are dealt. This is called the "ante" (pronounced "ant-tee"), and it buys you into the game. The dealer deals the cards, always starting with the player on her left and going clockwise. The number of cards depends on the game you are playing, but all final poker hands are based on five cards only.

The Deal

There are two main types of poker—stud and draw. In draw poker you are allowed to draw new cards after your initial hand is dealt, and your cards remain hidden from other players. In stud poker games, like Texas Hold 'Em, you cannot draw new cards, and some of your cards are played face up so the other players can see them. Both types can be played with either five cards or seven.

In the most common form of the game—five card draw—you will be dealt five cards facedown. The hands rank as follows (from highest to lowest):

Royal flush: Ace, king, queen, jack, and ten all of the same suit

Straight flush: Five cards of the same suit, in numerical sequence (e.g., two, three, four, five, and six of clubs)

Four of a kind: Four cards of the same face value (e.g., 4 fours)

Full house: Two cards of the same face value and three of another (e.g., 2 threes and 3 eights)

Flush: Five cards of the same suit but in no particular sequence (e.g., all hearts)

Straight: Five cards of different suits, in numerical sequence

Three of a kind: Three cards of the same face value (e.g., 3 aces)

Two pairs: Two sets of cards of the same face value (e.g., 2 queens and 2 tens)

One pair: Two cards of the same face value

Highest card: Hand is ranked only on the highest card held, usually an ace

If two or more players have the same hand, then the player with the highest-ranking cards wins.

The Bet ....

Each player looks at her cards and decides whether or not to stay in the game. If you choose to play, you must bet. You have several choices when it comes to betting:

Check. Hold off on making a bet and pass the bet to the next player. You can only do this if it's your turn first and no other players have made a bet.

See. Make a bet of the same amount as the bet made by the last player.

Raise. Raise the bet, forcing all other players to match your bet or raise the stakes higher.

Fold. Choose not to bet, turn in your cards, and forfeit your stake in the game.

If you stay in the game, you must match or raise not only the bet of the person who preceded you but all bets placed in that round, including the ones that are made after your bet. When you are making a bet, you must increase your original bet to match or raise the highest bet placed, regardless of who played first. For example, if player one bets $5, player two sees the bet (also bets $5), and player three raises the bet to $7, players one and two must increase their bets by $2 in order to stay in the game. You cannot bet less or choose not to bet at all, unless you are the first player and you choose to check. Most games have a limit on how much can be bet in a single round (for example, no more than $2 at a time) and on how many times the bet can be raised (for example, no more than three times in each round). You can choose to fold at anytime in the game.

The Draw ....

Once the first round of betting is complete, players may choose to exchange up to three cards with the dealer. Each player takes turns doing this, in the order in which the cards were dealt. This is called the "draw." The draw is blind,

meaning you cannot see the replacement cards before they are dealt.

Another round of betting follows the draw. Again, you can choose to fold, check, see, or raise. If all players see the bet (known as "calling" the bet), they enter into a showdown. Each player shows her cards and the highest hand wins. If only one player remains after the second round of betting—because all the other players have folded—she does not have to show her cards at all. This scenario happens most often in the case of a bluff.

The Bluff ....

If you have a weak hand but think you can bluff the other players into thinking otherwise, you can try to continue raising the bet until the other players drop out, believing your hand to be unbeatable. Bluffing is where you'll use your poker face, together with your knowledge of human body language. Commonly, players with a strong hand lean in toward their cards—they know they have a good chance of winning and are excited about their hand. Manipulate your own body language and study that of the other players, adjusting your own behavior accordingly.

As the song says, "You gotta know when to hold 'em, know when to fold 'em." On average, women win 15 percent more than men, just by knowing when to quit!

GIRL'S WORLD

Plan a poker night for your girl-friends. Buy poker chips, cards, pizza, beer, and soda and gamble until the wee hours.

Another watercooler headliner, fantasy football is exactly what it sounds like: an imaginary football team made up of the professional players of your choice, regardless of the teams they play for in real life. A fantasy football league runs for the entire NFL season, and points are accrued based on how well the real-life players do during the NFL season. Fantasy football is a long and complicated process, recommended only for the truly dedicated sports fan.

Joining a League and Forming a Team

Groups of friends or coworkers form fantasy football leagues, comprising eight to sixteen fantasy teams all competing against each other to win the league. Team owners (that's you and your friends) take turns selecting the players for their teams (the draft), until each owner has chosen a full team. To further complicate matters, you must choose not only your starting lineup but replacement players as well (in case real-life injury affects any of your fantasy team players). You can also make trades with other team owners throughout the season.

Picking Your Team

Most complete fantasy teams will include two quarterbacks, three wide receivers, two tight ends, one kicker, three running backs, and two defensive players. An active lineup can vary, but it often includes one quarterback, two running backs, two wide receivers, one tight end, and one defensive player. Fantasy teams include fewer players than regular NFL teams do.

Before the fantasy season begins, the number of play-off slots will be determined (based on your league size). The highest-scoring teams will compete in fantasy play-offs, which run concurrently with the last weeks of the NFL season.

You will pick your starting lineup from your pool of players each week, changing it as necessary over the course of the season to give your players the best matchups, or chance of winning, against other players in their real-life games and to accommodate injuries as they arise. All changes must be made prior to the real-life games in which the players in your lineup are competing that week.

Scoring Points ·················

The fantasy league rankings are based on points, with your players scoring points based on their performance in actual NFL games. The point system takes a bit of mastering, but this is the basic format:

- A touchdown is worth six points for the player who scores it. If the quarterback is involved in the play (by passing the ball to the scorer), he also wins six points.

- Kickers receive one fantasy football point for every actual extra point they score after a touchdown. Field goals are usually worth three points, but this can change depending on the length of the field goal. The longer the distance, the more points you get.

- All offensive players can gain points from receiving, rushing, and passing yardage. A common formula awards one point for every ten yards receiving or rushing and one point for every twenty-five yards of passing.

- Defensive players score points for tackles, sacks, and other defensive plays. A defensive touchdown is often worth more points than an offensive one.

- Players can lose points by fumbling the ball or throwing an interception.

The good news is that many Web sites are dedicated to fantasy football and will calculate all of these points for you, freeing you to concentrate on team management. Most leagues are tracked on Web sites, with team owners entering their picks at the beginning of the fantasy season and using the site to update their team and make changes.

Managing Your Team · · · · · · · · · · · ·

Here are some tips for getting your team to the fantasy league play-offs:

- When it's time to pick your players in the draft, be prepared. Fill out a cheat sheet (make your own or download one) to plan your optimum team, complete with backups in case you can't get your first choices.

- Learn the rules of your particular league thoroughly before picking your players, especially the ones governing how the draft works and how points are scored.

- Pick your running backs in the first two rounds. Most fantasy football fanatics agree that the strength of a team depends on running backs, since they have the potential to score the most points.

- Be flexible with your starting lineup and try to upgrade when possible. Remember to update your starting lineup on a weekly basis, to make sure you have the best team for your upcoming games.

- Prepare to make trades toward the end of the season if players are underperforming.

- Stick it out, even if your team is in a slump. Anything can happen, and at the very least you will be better prepared next year!

If all else fails, choose your players based on which players have the nicest butts. Not only will you have something fun to look at all season, but if your nice-butt team triumphs in the fantasy bowl your male competitors will be more than a little irritated.

GIRL'S WORLD

You can form a fantasy sports league for pretty much any team sport. Why not create a league for women's soccer and invite your sports-crazy girlfriends to compete?

The Jargon

Cheat sheet: A spreadsheet ranking players by their fantasy scoring abilities; an essential tool for making draft picks

Depth chart: A list of all the players on your team, ranked from best to worst

Sleeper: A player who didn't perform well in the previous season, but is expected to improve in the next season; often great draft picks

I Can . . . Arm Wrestle!

Arm wrestling may not be the most feminine activity, and it's definitely not one that most women are especially physically equipped for, but not getting your ass kicked at arm wrestling is still a great party trick. The good news is that sheer strength is not the only road to arm-wrestling victory. If you can master the technique and build your speed, you may surprise yourself (and others).

The Rules

The rules are pretty simple:

- Two competitors must face each other across a table, either standing or sitting. Standing is better.

- One elbow (and nothing else) is on the table and must remain on the table at all times. Lifting your elbow from the table is considered a foul.

- No part of your body may touch your hand at any time.

- You win the game when you cause any part of your competitor's hand or arm to touch the table.

- Loud groaning is acceptable and encouraged.

The Moves

There are three common arm wrestling moves: the top roll, the hook, and the press.

The top roll. The most glamorous of the three moves, the top roll is a great one for women because it relies more on leverage than on strength. Assess your opponent's strength—if your opponent looks bigger or stronger than you, then the top roll is probably your best bet. Immortalized in the Sylvester Stallone classic *Over the Top*, the trick is to put as much pressure as you can on your opponent's fingers by rolling your hand on top of your opponent's and positioning your hand so that your wrist is above his fingers and his wrist is bent back. The goal is to force him to open his fingers, providing you with the opportunity to push his hand to the table. Once the hand is opened, you must strengthen your own hand position and go in for the kill. For a successful top roll, pull your opponent's arm toward you. The top roll is known as an "outside" move, because it focuses on your opponent's hand instead of his arm.

The hook. Considered an "inside" move, the hook aims to beat the arm and not the hand. Since it requires a stronger arm than that of your opponent, this one may be more difficult if you're playing with a guy. If you decide on the hook, use the element of speed to your advantage and go for the takedown as soon as the match begins. Keep your arm close to your body and curl your wrist as much as you can. Push down using the full strength of your body, not just your arm. Not utilizing your full body strength is a very common mistake. As long as your body doesn't touch your hand you can lean in as close as you want. If your opponent tries to hook you, try to switch to the top roll.

The press. This move relies on sheer power. Try to get your opponent's palm to face up, placing your own hand on top of his. Then position your body above the arm so you can push down and, as the name suggests, press to the table. As with the hook, if your opponent tries this move on you, switch to the top roll and try to pull his arm toward you. This should help shut down the press and throw him off guard.

Remember the following key points the next time you go "over the top":

- If standing, position your feet so that the foot on the same side as your wrestling arm is in front.

- Utilize your full body strength to pressure his arm to the table.

- Keep your own arm as close to your body as possible. If your opponent manages to pull your arm toward him, you will lose your ability to use your full body strength.

Random Fact: There is evidence of arm wrestling dating back to the ancient Egyptians. However, the modern sport is based on a Native American game.

I Can . . . Shoot a Free Throw!

Few things will make you look more like a total sports stud than shooting a fifteen-foot free throw clean into the basket. Use the tips below to turn your occasional fluke shot into a regular occurrence.

Get in Position

To start, make sure your feet are parallel and shoulder-width apart. Stand a few inches back from the free-throw line, in case you need to take a little jump when you throw the ball. Place your dominant foot (the right foot, for most of us) so it lines up directly with the net; this will help you aim straight for the basket. Many free-throw lines have a small mark painted on the court indicating the center of the net. Your dominant foot should be in line with this mark. Some people like to have one foot slightly behind the other. Find the most comfortable position for you.

Position the Ball

How you hold the ball will make or break your shot. Simply launching it with all your might in the direction of the net will get you nowhere. Place the ball in your dominant hand and bend your hand back until your wrist creases. Raise the ball to shoulder height, and pull your elbow in as far as is comfortable. You should be holding the ball with your fingers, not your palm. Support the ball with your other hand.

Get in the Zone

The free throw is basketball's most nerve-wracking shot. As you approach the line, take a few deep breaths. Try to block out all background noise and concentrate on getting the ball into the net.

Experts recommend that you follow the same routine every time—dribble the ball three times and then shoot, for example. This will help you remain calm and consistent. Visualize the ball going into the net as you take your shot.

Make Your Shot ·················

Bend your knees slightly as you prepare to shoot. When you're ready, you'll bend them slightly more and push up. Aim for the square painted on the backboard (aiming too short is a common error). Straighten your legs as you straighten your arm, using your legs for most of the power. You can jump a little or keep both feet firmly on the ground, whichever is most comfortable for you—just don't step over the free-throw line. Now, shoot! Follow through with your shooting arm, as if you are reaching straight for the net, and release the ball from your fingertips to create backspin.

Practice Like a Crazy Person ·····

You need to practice this one—a lot.
Develop your own routine and find the
position that is most comfortable for you.
You will be more consistent if you always
shoot in the same way. Start closer to the
net and keep working your way backward
until you can make a shot from the free-
throw line with ease.

Learning to shoot a free throw could turn
out to be a meditative experience. It's as
much about having the right mind-set as
having the right technique. With enough
practice, your shots will soon be nothin'
but net!

I Can ... Talk Sports!

Anywhere men congregate there is sports talk, and often sports arguments and even sports bets. Sports can be described as the male outlet for human drama. Instead of discussing relationships between people they know, they watch the heartache, the tension, and the triumph unfold on the sports field. Acquiring an insane amount of knowledge about your local sports teams is an essential part of participating in the male world and one rarely mastered by women.

When, Where, and Why

Sports talk falls into one of two categories. The first is general sports talk and debate, to be used when you run out of more interesting things to talk about, or when you want to shock a group of guys with your expert knowledge and passion. The second—a little more lively and interactive—is game-watching armchair commentary, during which you can shout, swear, curse, and cheer with abandon while shouting instructions at the television. Yes, we know the players can't hear you.

You will find many opportunities throughout the year to use your sports talk, particularly around the Super Bowl, the World Series, the World Cup (every four years), the NBA Championships, or any play-off game leading up to a major tournament. Pretty much any sport can provide fodder for endless speculation and armchair yelling, except perhaps figure skating and lawn bowling.

Talk the Talk ·

True sports fans are geeks at heart. They can rattle off facts and figures at will and seem to have an endless capacity for remembering the details of bygone games. Guys have been training for this since birth, so unless you plan to do some serious studying, you'll need to fake it. Here's how:

• Start by picking your sport and your team (we recommend choosing the local franchise). Then do some Internet research on the team you will be supporting.

• Know the key players and their basic statistics. If you're talking about a baseball team, you'll need to study ERA or batting averages; for football, focus on quarterback statistics like completion percentage (see "The Jargon" on page 40). That being said, don't get too hung up on this stuff. Most guys don't know too much about stats that go beyond the obvious:

general historical dominance, results, league standings. Memorizing one or two will set you on a par with most men and make you a tough opponent in a sports debate.

• Don't forget to learn the names of the managers, coaches, and team owners—this is absolutely essential. Being able to mention the name of the coach in conversation goes a long way toward making you look like a true fan.

• Keep up to date with your team's performance in the run up to the big game, both on the road and at home. The end of the season is when sports get truly exciting and sports talk reaches its zenith.

• Listen to sports talk radio in the car. This is a quick and easy way to learn some good catchphrases and factoids.

• Find a sports pundit you like and read his (or her) stuff. If he (or she) proves consistently correct, you can borrow his (or her) opinions and toss them out in conversation.

- Many sports debates focus on the subject of who is the best quarterback (or pitcher, or coach) of all time and why. You can join this debate without using too many real facts—just be prepared to fight tooth and nail for your nominee. And be sure to pick someone who fits pretty well into the category.

- Research a couple of specific historical facts about your team so you can say things such as "It's like 1967 all over again." Guys will avoid challenging you, for fear of being shown up by your superior knowledge.

- Pay attention during the game and remember a few details to discuss in the post-game analysis. Remembering a play from the first quarter and reliving it after the game is a sign of a true fan. If you worry about saying the wrong thing, try to remember a statement made by the commentator and use it as your own.

Yell the Yell ·

Yelling at the TV is a great way to let off some steam. The rules of "Talk the Talk" still apply, but here you get to do it with more gusto.

- You should be wearing some kind of sports attire, drinking a beer, and eating chips or peanuts. The sports attire should match the team you are supporting, not your shoes.

- Shouting instructions at the television is mandatory. This could be a simple phrase, like "Hustle" or "Catch that!" or something more complex, like "Nice play, [insert surname]," followed by loud clapping. You can also go negative: "What the hell was that?" Used often and correctly, this will make you look like a true aficionado. Follow the commentary on the TV for guidance.

- When your team is doing well, feel free to cheer, clap, and jump out of your chair. Also feel free to swear at and insult the opposing team and any fans of the opposing team who happen to be around. If your team is not doing so well, you must swear at and insult your own team.

- If your team is performing *really* terribly in a crucial game, try covering your eyes while holding your head in your hands. If they actually lose said crucial game, you must remain speechless for a short period of time before you start your post-game analysis.

- Be prepared to argue drunkenly at any opportunity in defense of your team. In this type of situation, loudness can easily make up for lack of information.

The Jargon

Earned Run Average (ERA): The average number of runs a pitcher allows in a game. ("Our pitching is an embarrassment this year. Can you believe this 8.9 ERA crap?")

Runs Batted In (RBI): The amount of runs scored as the result of a particular batter's hits. ("Garcia has some real pop in his bat this season—23 RBIs ain't bad.")

Passer Rating: A super-complicated NFL formula for rating quarterbacks. It's based on completed passes, pass attempts, passes resulting in touchdowns, and intercepted passes. ("McBride's passer rating is the second highest in the NFL this year.")

Most Valuable Player (MVP): A title given to the best-performing player in a particular league, team, or series of games. ("Daly totally deserved to be MVP. He was robbed.")

I Can . . . Win at the Track!

A day at the races is always a ton of fun, but it is even better if you walk away with cold, hard cash. You can bet on horse racing online, but going to the track to watch the race and cheer on your horse is a great way to spend a sunny afternoon.

Study the Form

When you get to the track, the first thing you will want to do is pick up a copy of the racing form, provided free of charge, which gives details on the horses racing that day as well as the condition of the track. The racing form will tell you everything you need to know about each horse (age, weight, height, and so on) and its performances in previous races—the length of the horse's races, how much the horse has won by (if at all), the number of races it has run so far in its career, and its performance on similar tracks. It will also give you each horse's odds of winning that day, according to the bookmakers.

By studying the form, you can make some educated guesses about which horses have a chance of winning. Pay close attention to how long the race is (horse races are measured in furlongs, equal to one-eighth of a mile) and how your horse has fared in races of this distance and on tracks of a similar condition. Check the bookies' odds on each horse—a horse with 2:1 odds is usually the favorite to win, while a horse at 20:1 is considered a long shot. However, anything can happen at the track, so have some fun betting on a variety of favorites as well as some "dark horses." Your odds of winning may go down, but if you pick correctly you stand to win a lot more money.

Place Your Bets ················

Once you have chosen your winners, go to the cashier's window and place your first bet. You should wait until the last possible minute to place your bet—the odds set by the bookmakers change as more bets are placed, so waiting it out will give you the most accurate information. There are a number of ways to bet on a horse. Tell the cashier which type of bet you are placing:

To win: This means you're betting that your chosen horse will come in first.

To place: You're betting that your horse will come in first or second.

To show: You're betting that your horse will finish first, second, or third.

Exacta: You choose the two horses that you think will finish first and second, in the correct order.

Trifecta: You choose the three horses that will finish first, second, and third, in the correct order.

Obviously, the amount you win varies according to which type of bet you place—if you bet "to win" you stand to make more than if you bet "to show," since your odds of winning are slimmer. You can usually bet as little as a dollar per race. Keep your ticket, because you will need it to claim your winnings. Once you've placed your bet, return to the stands to cheer on your horse. If you

2 Careless Miss	C.d.3		Life	17 5 4 1	$229,400 101	D. Fst	1 1 0 0 $22,800 97
Own: Charles L. Heekin	Sire: Staunch Avenger $50,000		2001	1 0 0 1	$5,330 97	Wet(312) 0 0 0 0 $0 —
Pink, Green Sash, Green Sleeves	Dam: Miss Colarts		2000	5 2 0 0	$82,800 101	Turf(205) 16 4 4 1 $206,600 101
ARCARO EDDIE (159 40 31 26 .25)	Br: Charles L Heekin	L116	GP	3 2 0 1	$185,330 101	Dist	2 1 0 0 $120,000 100
	Tr: Sherrill Ward (92 22 18 19 .24)						

win, bring your ticket to the cashier's window to collect your winnings. If you lose, rip up your ticket and stomp on it before returning to the window to place your next bet!

The Jargon

Classic: A well-known and important race such as the Kentucky Derby

Triple Crown: The three major races in the United States— the Kentucky Derby, the Preakness Stakes, and the Belmont Stakes

Filly: A female horse four years old or younger

Gelding: A castrated male horse

Mare: A female horse over five years, or any female horse that has been bred

Invented in the medieval times to help archers practice their aim (the original dartboard was the bottom of a barrel), today's game is more often played in your local pub. While the combination of drinking and throwing sharp objects may sound somewhat risky, we are sure that once you get the hang of it, all of your throws will at least make it to the board.

Setup and Equipment

To be a true dart aficionado, you should invest in the proper equipment. Pick up an inexpensive set of darts (usually around $20 to $25 for a first set, although they can get significantly more expensive) and a dartboard (around $25) so you can practice at home. Go to a proper sporting goods or games store and test out a few different types of darts, focusing on three main factors: weight, length, and grip. You may find that your preferences change as your throw develops (the harder you throw, the heavier your dart should be), so we recommend not spending too much in the beginning. The standard height for a dartboard is 5 feet 8 inches from the floor to the center of the bull's-eye, and the throwing line should be 7 feet 9 inches from the face of the board (not the wall).

The Throw

In a throw, the dart travels along a curve—starting low, heading upward, and then curving back down as it loses speed. As you'll soon discover, your throwing skill is the most important aspect of the game.

When you're ready to throw, you first need to aim, focusing on the board and nothing else. Line the dart up with your eye, and your eye with the section of the board you're aiming for. Pull your arm back and release the dart toward the board, following through with your whole arm. Keep in mind that the only part of your body that should move during the throw is your arm. The rest of your body, including your shoulder, should remain stable. The dart should start its flight aiming slightly upward, following the natural curve of your arm motion. If you throw in a downward motion, you will miss the board and will most likely hit someone's foot.

Tips for Aiming

- Develop a stance you are comfortable with and always use that same stance. This will reduce variability and make your throw more consistent.

- Practice throwing a smooth and natural curve.

- Pick a point on the dart to aim with; the tip works well in most cases.

The Game ······················

Darts is played by two people or two teams. Several practice shots are allowed for each player before the game begins. To determine who goes first, each player, or a member of each team, throws an initial dart. The player whose dart lands closest to the bull's-eye goes first.

The most common game in darts (and the game played by professionals) is called "501" or "301." Each player starts with 501 points (or 301 for a shorter game). You must throw a double of any number (read on for an explanation of doubles and triples) before you can start to score. Three darts are thrown by each player per turn, and the points scored are deducted from 501, the winner being the first to reach zero. Which leads us to the second most important skill in darts: math! You must be able to add up your score and deduct it from your total with relative ease. Since the game includes triple and double scoring, this can get tricky—triple 16, plus double 9, plus triple 19 subtracted from 425? Anyone? Anyone?

The bull's-eye is worth 50 points, the outer ring of the bull's-eye is worth 25 points, and the numbered segments (one through twenty) are scored according to their assigned numbers. However, each numbered segment has a double and triple ring, which are worth double or triple the points. Therefore, the highest single throw in darts is not the bull's-eye, but a triple 20, worth 60 points. If you watch a professional darts match, you will notice that the players try to score triple 20 with each dart, for a maximum score of 180 per turn.

To finish the game you must score exactly zero, and you must go out on a double. For example, if you have 10 points remaining you must throw a double 5 to win. Say you miss the double 5 and hit the double 1—your total score is now 8 and you must throw a double 4 to win, and so on. If you go over your remaining score (by throwing a double 6 or a single 16, for example) or if you

reduce your score to 1 and are therefore unable to go out on a double, your turn is considered a bust. In this case, you keep the points you started the turn with (10 points in our example) and try to finish on a double in your next turn.

Another common darts game (more suitable for the mathematically challenged) is Around the Clock. In Around the Clock, each player must hit each number in order, starting with 1 and finishing with the outer bull and then the bull's-eye. As in 501, you throw three darts per turn, but you cannot move on to the next number until you have successfully hit the number you are aiming for. Around the Clock is a great game to play by yourself, to practice your aim.

Darts is a great game with plenty of perks: With practice, women have the same chance of winning darts as men do. Plus, it's addictive, you don't have to be physically fit, and it is cheap to play. Best of all, it's most often accompanied by a pint of beer. What could be better than that? Make darts your game, but try not to develop the massive beer belly of most professional darts players.

If your father spent every Sunday morning playing golf, every Sunday lunch talking about golf, and every Sunday afternoon napping on the couch while ostensibly watching golf on television, then we don't need to tell you that men who play golf are hopeless addicts. Nowadays, however, women are taking up the sport in increasing numbers (maybe so they won't have to spend their retirements alone) and female professional golfers are getting more press coverage than ever before.

The golf course is not just a place for wearing plaid pants and white shoes; it can also be a place for networking and business bonding. The golf course is one of the last bastions of gender segregation—some clubs do not allow women to play at all, while others restrict women to specific time slots. Afraid of being shown up, perhaps?

The Game

The game of golf involves hitting a small white ball into a faraway hole using the smallest number of shots (strokes) possible. You play either nine or eighteen holes, and your shots accumulate as you move from one hole to the next. Each hole has a "par," the ideal number of strokes in which to complete the hole. If you get anywhere near par, you are a golf stud.

Most golfers will tell you that the hardest shot to hit well is the first shot of each hole, also known as the "tee shot." (In golf, *tee* means the location from which you hit the ball at the beginning of a hole.) If you can hit a good tee shot, you will be well set up for the rest of the hole. Most courses have different tees for women, which are slightly closer to the hole, compensating for women's slight strength disadvantage.

The Right Club

In order to hit your perfect tee shot, you first need to choose the right club for the job. A longer shot requires a longer club, usually a wood, like a driver. But longer clubs are also less accurate. When you first start to play golf, you should be going for accuracy over distance. Resist the temptation to use the big stick, and start with an iron. Work your way up as your game improves.

The Right Stance

The key to the proper golf stance is balance. Stand parallel to the target line—in other words, with the side of your body facing the direction in which you are hitting the ball. Your feet should be placed shoulder-width apart, on either side of the ball. Stand about 2 feet back from the ball.

The Right Grip

The directions below are written for right-handed players; simply reverse them if you're left handed.

1. Standing in the stance described previously, place the club head on the ground, with both hands on the grip at the top of the club.

2. Remove your right hand and adjust your left hand so you are holding the club with your fingers, not your palm. The thumb of your left hand should be parallel with the shaft, pointing straight down the grip, toward the ground.

3. Now, place the fingers of your right hand on the grip, fingers at the back, below the fingers of your left hand.

4. Wrap your right hand around the grip, with the palm of your right hand slightly overlapping your left thumb. Your right thumb should not be facing straight down the shaft, but slightly angled toward your left foot.

5. Hold the club with a light, yet controlled, grip.

The Right Swing · · · · · · · · · · · · · · · ·

Now that you have the club, the stance, and the grip, it is time to head to the driving range and practice your swing. Please keep in mind that when you start trying to hit balls, you will suck. It is inevitable.

A golf swing can be broken down into four stages:

1. **The backswing** happens when you swing the club behind you in order to hit the ball. Your left arm should be as straight as possible, and your right elbow should be bent at about 90 degrees when you reach the top of your backswing. Keep your head still and your eye on the ball.

2. **The downswing** is the motion of the club swinging down toward the ball. Your knees, thighs, and hips move forward (but your feet are still) as the club swings. Keep your head still and your eye on the ball.

3. **The point of impact** is when the club hits the ball. At this point the left (front) arm and the club should form a continuous straight line. Your weight should be slightly forward on the outside edge of the front foot and the inside of the back foot, with the heel of your back foot raised off the ground. Keep your head still and your eye on the ball.

4. **The follow-through** occurs when you swing the club forward once the ball is struck. The club head ends up behind your left shoulder, as your left wrist rotates back and your elbows bend. Your weight should be on the front foot, with only the toes of your back foot on the ground.

Obviously there is a lot more to the game of golf than your tee shot. May we suggest getting an attractive young golf pro to show you the finer points of the game?

The Jargon

Wood: A club used for driving the ball long distances. The most common woods are the driver, the 3 wood, and the 5 wood.

Iron: Any of a variety of iron clubs used for medium distances. Most beginners will only need the irons numbered 5 to 9.

Wedge: A club used to play shorter shots that require "loft," or height, such as getting out of a sand trap

Putter: The club used on the green to "putt" the ball short distances into the hole

I Can... Throw a Baseball!

It seems that everyone had that draconian (not to mention chauvinistic) high school PE teacher who accused the boys of "throwing like a girl." Well, with a little help from us, you can start turning that old school insult into a major compliment.

The ability to throw a ball accurately, with speed and strength, is as essential to the games of baseball and softball as the ability to hit the ball when at bat. Throwing the ball is a skill required of all positions on the field, not just the pitcher. Although a good throw involves your whole body, the first step is to develop a strong grip.

The Grip

The red stitching on a baseball is not just for decoration. As you hold the ball, you'll see a seam that forms a shape similar to that of a peanut. You want to hold the ball so your fingers lie across, not parallel to, the two seams. Hold the ball mostly with your fingers and less with your palm.

You'll need a different grip if you want to try pitching some fancy throws such as curveballs or knuckleballs, but for your basic, all-purpose throw, this is the grip you will need to use.

The Throw

The first part of your body to focus on is your wrist. Your wrist is like the trigger for the throw, which means you'll cock it back and use it to help propel the ball when you make your throw. Make sure your wrist is not stiff. Ideally, the ball will be rotating in a perfect circle as it spins through the air.

The next important body part is, not surprisingly, your arm. All throwing should consist of a circular motion of the arm—the circle may expand and decrease with the distance of the throw, but it still forms a circle nonetheless. You'll start with your arm behind you and move it upward in a wide arc. Keep it moving downward in front of you, and release the ball, propelling it with your wrist and shoulder, when your hand passes the apex of the arc. For longer throws, start with your hand a little lower behind you.

The final aspect to think about is your body position. Arrange your entire body so it is sideways to the target of your throw. Step off from your back foot (your right foot if you are throwing right-handed), leaning forward onto your front foot as you throw. This will ensure that your whole body strength is behind the throw.

Now, put all three body movements together, and practice! At your next company ball game, you'll be able to strut out to the outfield while confidently assuring your teammates that they needn't worry—you throw like a girl, after all!

The Jargon

Curveball: A ball thrown so it curves in the air and is therefore harder to hit

Knuckleball: A slow pitch thrown with the knuckles or fingertips, making the ball's path hard to predict

Fastball: A ball thrown straight and fast

Slider: A fast pitch that curves slightly in the opposite direction from the pitcher's arm as it nears the bat

I Can ... Shoot Craps!

Craps is the liveliest game in any casino. The table is almost always surrounded with people cheering the shooter on as he throws the dice on the table. If you want to be the center of attention as the shooter, and not just the hot chick who gets to blow on the dice for luck, read on.

At first the rules of craps can seem confusing and overwhelming, but it pays off to persevere, since the return on your bets can be very good. However, if you approach a craps table without a basic understanding of the game, you may get swept up in the excitement and lose your money in the first five minutes.

Craps is a fast-moving game played with two regular, six-sided dice. Up to sixteen people can play at any one time, hence the noise and chaos. Basically, the object of the game is to predict the roll of the dice. You bet with or against the shooter, and you win or lose based on the sum of the numbers on the dice.

The Shooter

Each player takes turns being the shooter, but you can opt to pass on your turn if you prefer. However, passing is lame and no fun, so when your turn rolls around, go for it. Here is what you need to know when shooting:

1. The shooter must place a bet before rolling the dice.

2. The shooter then chooses two dice to throw from the selection offered. Despite all those old movies you've seen where glamorous starlets blow on dice for good luck, it goes against casino etiquette to kiss or blow on the dice.

3. Holding the dice in one hand only, the shooter throws the dice hard down the table, so they ricochet off the guard at the end of the table. This is done to ensure that the shooter cannot really control the throw of the dice. The face-up numbers on the dice are added together to determine the value of the throw.

4. The first throw the shooter makes, called the "come-out roll," is the most important throw of the shooter's turn. There are three possible throws:

- **The natural** is a throw of 7 or 11. If the shooter rolls either 7 or 11, she automatically wins.

- **Craps** means a roll of 2, 3, or 12. If the shooter rolls one of these three totals, she loses, or "craps out."

- **Points** is a roll of any of the other numbers, 4, 5, 6, 8, 9, or 10. If the shooter rolls a point in her come-out roll, then in order to win she must roll that same number again before she rolls a 7. If she rolls 7 before she rolls her original point, she loses. For example, if the come-out roll is a 5, the shooter continues to roll until she rolls either another 5 (she wins the point) or a 7 (she loses).

5. If you roll the natural, roll craps, or make a point, then you can carry on rolling the dice. If you lose on the point, your turn ends and you must pass the dice to the next player. You can also choose to pass at any time once the point has been made.

The Gambler · · · · · · · · · · · · · · · · · · ·

The other players at the table are also betting on the game. You choose whether to bet with or against the shooter. The most common bets are the following:

Pass-line bet. You are betting that either the shooter will roll 7 or 11 on the first roll or if she rolls a point, that she will then roll the same point before rolling a 7. If she craps out on the first throw, you lose. Likewise, if she rolls a point but then rolls a 7 before rolling the established point, you also lose. The odds are even on pass-line bets, meaning you stand to double your money. Place your chips next to the pass line on the table to make this bet.

Don't-pass bet. Here, you are betting the opposite of the pass line. You are hoping for a 2, 3, or 12 on the first throw, or a point followed by a 7 before the point number is rolled. Basically, you want the shooter to lose. If the shooter doesn't lose, you do. Don't-pass bets also pay even odds.

Place bet. In this bet, you are betting that the shooter will roll a 4, 5, 6, 8, 9, or 10 before she rolls a 7. The odds depend on which number you bet on.

For example, the odds are higher for a 4 than an 8, since the chance of rolling a 4 is less than the chance of rolling an 8.

Quite a few other bets are used in craps, but the three listed above are the easiest to understand and the safest to place. Next time you hit Vegas, find out what it's like to be a high roller!

The Jargon

Snake eyes: A roll of two 1s

Back line: Another term for the don't-pass bet

Bones: A nickname for dice

Wrong bettor: A player who bets against the dice

Are You a Sports Fanatic or a Sports Flunky?

1. The term *March Madness* refers to

   a. The major tournament of the NCAA basketball season

   b. The major tournament of the NBA basketball season

   c. The major debut of the NBC spring lineup

2. The highest hand in poker is

   a. A royal flush

   b. Aces high

   c. A toilet flush

3. In golf, you usually hit a tee shot with

   a. A wood

   b. An iron

   c. A baseball bat

4. If you roll a 2, 3, or 12 on your come-out throw in craps, you

   a. Crap out

   b. Seven out

   c. Are crap

5. The infield-fly rule prevents

   a. An easy double play

   b. A pop-up

   c. A player's pants from falling down

Mostly *A*'s: She shoots, she scores!

You have grasped the finer points of the games and are ready to take on the boys at their own game—and win!

Mostly *B*'s: She shoots, she nearly scores!

You mean well, and you're an enthusiastic sports faker, but you may never have the attention span to be a true sportsaholic.

Mostly *C*'s: She shoots, she misses by 10 feet!

You have never even watched a football game, let alone had a conversation about it. We recommend that you develop your skills before someone loses an eye in a darts game.

My Way

Let's take a second to congratulate ourselves. Over the last forty years women have made incredible advances in every imaginable area of life. There are female astronauts and scientists, senators and ambassadors, CEOs and CPAs, and everything in between. However, as we all know, women still receive lower pay than their male counterparts do for comparable work, and few women hold top executive positions. We have yet to nominate a female for president, let alone see one in office. Looks like we have work to do!

Male attitudes and styles still dominate the workplace. While a more feminine model of leadership is starting to be recognized—and we're seeing corresponding positive changes such as increased teamwork and flexible schedules—when it comes to getting to the top, the guys still seem to have the edge.

Okay, so you don't want to be a big jerk. But there's a lot you can learn from the guys. For many women, the problem is simple: We are too nice and too selfless. We often worry that our success will come at the expense of others—our children's happiness, our spouses' egos, our colleagues' feelings—and this prevents us from going all out to get the things we want. Well, now's the time to stop our fussing. We know we wouldn't be able to make everybody happy even if we did sacrifice our careers. If we succeed on the job, *we'll* be happy, at least.

This chapter is designed to boost your confidence and teach you some of the skills that successful men use to get ahead. Once you develop your new skill set, you can start putting your newfound confidence to work. Total world domination is only a few pages away!

I Can . . . *Ask for a Raise!*

Research suggests that women lose hundreds of thousands of dollars over the course of their careers by neglecting to ask for raises and failing to negotiate for a higher salary when accepting a new job. That's right, *hundreds of thousands of dollars!* That sucks. Not only does it suck, but it is also entirely avoidable.

Notice Me! ·

You are kicking butt at your job, your job description is expanding, and so is your level of responsibility. In fact, pretty much everything is expanding except your bank balance. Your performance review is around the corner and your supervisors are planning to offer you the standard 2 percent cost-of-living increase. In past years you have accepted this, believing that they must have noticed how hard you work and would reward you if they could. Wrong! Think about it—why on earth would a company spontaneously decide to give money to people who haven't asked for it?

Show Me the Money! · · · · · · · · · · · ·

Follow these simple steps, and see your salary (and ego) grow.

Be clear about what you want. Search the Internet to find out what other companies in your area pay for the same type of job. Come up with a number that you think is fair, based on your responsibilities and experience. Be realistic, but don't sell yourself short. A good rule is to ask for 2 percent more than you would be happy with. For example, if you earn $50,000 a year and would like a raise of 10 percent, or $5,000, ask for 12 percent, or $6,000.

Write your own performance review.
Prepare a description of your current
duties, what you have accomplished
since you took the job, how your position
has grown, your major achievements,
and your future goals. Don't be afraid
to brag, but do make sure you can sub-
stantiate all of your claims.

Pick a good time. Schedule a meeting
with your boss several days in advance.
Don't spring it on her in the elevator, or
over an impromptu lunch. If she is in
the middle of a particularly hectic week,
you may want to wait until a better time.
That said, if no time is ever a good time,
then just schedule your meeting to discuss your raise as soon as is reasonable.

Be confident, prepared, and calm. Role-
play all of the scenarios with a friend
ahead of time so you feel prepared.
When you meet with your boss, present
your written materials and listen to her
response. Let her make you an offer first,
in case she has a higher number in mind
than you are planning to ask for. Be
ready to negotiate (see "I Can . . .

Negotiate!" page 72), since you might not
get exactly what you want.

Be prepared to take no for an answer.
Before making your big request, think
about other forms of compensation you
could be happy with in the short term,
if they're unable to give you a monetary
raise right away. Could they offer extra
vacation days, a flexible work schedule,
or other benefits instead? If they don't
think you are ready for a promotion, ask
them to help you work out a plan to get
you where you want to be within a set
amount of time. If they just refuse to
budge, then you may need to think about
a change of jobs, since there is obviously
no room for growth where you are.

Don't Be a Dummy ··············

Part of being prepared is knowing what
not to do. As tempting as they may seem,
avoid these common mistakes:

*   Don't be a baby. No pleading, crying,
    or yelling allowed.

- Don't be unprofessional. You get a raise based on your performance, not because you can't pay your rent or your credit card bill is sky high. Avoid making personal statements.

- Don't compare yourself to your coworkers. The fact that you do ten times more than Rich in the cube next to yours is not relevant. Focus on how great you are, not on how bad others may be.

- Don't bluff unless you can back it up. Stating that you have an offer from another company is one of the best ways to get a raise. Threatening to leave when you have nowhere to go is not.

- Don't feel sorry for your employer. Women often suffer from misplaced sympathies. This is business. If they genuinely can't afford it, they will let you know.

If you don't ask, the answer is always no. It is better to ask and be turned down than to not ask at all just because it seems scary, uncomfortable, or awkward. This is your life we are talking about—your security, your children's education, your two weeks in Thailand! Have a vision in mind of what you need that money for and use it to give you the courage to ask for what you deserve.

GIRL'S WORLD

This year, make a pact with a few close friends to go for the gold at your annual reviews. Help each other benchmark the market, brainstorm strategies for approaching the boss, and rehearse various scenarios. When you get your big fat raise, throw a party to celebrate your success. If you ask for that big fat raise and your company turns you down flat, throw a party to celebrate quitting your job!

I Can . . . Buy a Car!

Owning a new car is exhilarating, but buying a new car can be frustrating, confusing, and stressful. Despite the fact that women comprise the fastest-growing segment of the car-buying market, many still assume that they'll be treated unfairly by car dealers and will end up paying too much. However, if you enter the situation thoroughly prepared, there is no reason why you shouldn't drive off the lot with the deal of the year.

One of the major problems with the hard sell is that it's almost impossible to know when you are getting the best deal. You just can't shake the feeling that you are being ripped off, even if you are not. The only way to avoid this is to do your homework ahead of time.

Firm Up Your Financing

Before you go anywhere near a dealership, you need to get your finances in order. Here's how to do it:

- Work out a budget. Decide how much you will pay up front, and how much you can afford to pay on a monthly basis. Don't forget to include interest rates, taxes, and insurance. When you total up all the related expenses, a new car often costs a lot more than the advertised price.

- Obtain your credit report. If your credit is bad, you will have a hard time getting a good deal on financing and may need to look at other options.

- Shop for financing. This is one of the best ways to lower your car payments. Check with several banks or credit unions to see what interest rates they will offer you on a loan. Then, when you're negotiating with the car salesperson, you can use the backup deal from the bank to finagle an even lower interest rate from the dealership. If they can't match the rate from the bank, then you'll know you got the best financing available.

Find Your Price

Once you have decided which car you can afford to buy and have gone on several test drives at a number of dealers, you need to decide on your price. Because this price will be your non-negotiable number, it needs to be fair, realistic, and accurate.

Start by finding out the invoice price of the particular make and model you are planning to buy—the price the dealer paid the manufacturer for the car. This price will be lower than the sticker price, also called the "manufacturer's suggested retail price" (MSRP), which includes dealer markup.

Determining the invoice price at the dealership can be more complicated than you think—many of the items they list as part of the "factory" or invoice price include additional options you may not want, or costs that are actually refunded to the dealer by the manufacturer, like transportation. Dealers also don't include bonuses that the manufacturer pays to the dealer—these can represent thousands of dollars in additional profit. The best way to figure out a fair invoice price is to go to a Web site that specializes in providing this type of information. You may have to pay a small fee for the info, but it could save you thousands in the long run.

Once you know the invoice price, you know the actual value of the car. No dealer will sell a car for the invoice price—after all, they do need to make some profit in order to stay in business. A reasonable offer would include both the invoice price and a fair profit for the dealer. If you want to drive a hard bargain, offer 5 percent over the invoice price.

Obtain quotes on your car of choice, including any options you want (such as a sun roof or CD player), from online dealers. If you are not comfortable making such a large purchase online, you can bring your various electronic offers with you to the dealership to use in your negotiations. Having in hand a better offer from another dealer is one of the best ways to bring down the price.

Make a Deal ·

Before you go, you should also familiarize yourself with the kinds of paperwork you will be shown at the dealership. The forms will vary according to the type of deal you are negotiating and the state where you live. Check consumer rights Web sites for explanations of the key terms you'll need to know. If you understand all of the terms, you won't be easily intimidated.

Now, it's off to the dealership to make the deal. You want to look like you mean business, which you do, so bring all of your documentation with you—your credit reports, financing plan, research materials, and offers from online dealers. This way, you'll have the documents to back you up during negotiations.

Dealing with the salespeople is the biggest challenge. If you can see it as a game instead of a traumatic experience, you will be much better off. Keep these tips in mind and prepare to be tough:

- Set a time limit and stick to it. Tell them that you have only thirty minutes to close the deal. This should cut down on the old "I need to talk to my manager" trick, which can go on forever, while you sit there sweating it out.

- Don't go alone. Bring a friend or family member with you. It will boost your confidence to have someone there on your side.

- Be prepared to deal with sales tactics. Common ones include "I can sell this car to someone else at full price, so why should we sell it to you for less?" and "This deal ends tomorrow." Don't believe it!

- Don't feel sorry for the salespeople. They can make money from all the other suckers—but not from you!

- Have confidence in your offer. You have done your research and know that you are offering a fair deal. Tell them what you are willing to pay and refuse to be swayed.

- Decide what options you want, and factor those into your nonnegotiable price, before you start your negotiations. Many options offered, such as car alarms or fabric protection, can be obtained elsewhere for less.

- Be ready to walk away. If you are not prepared to leave empty handed, they have already won.

Negotiating with a car dealer is one of the toughest transactions in the business world. But, at the end of the day, they want your money. Ultimately, you are the one with the upper hand.

Faking It!

Make the salesperson sweat it instead of you. Walk confidently around the vehicle for a long time, inspecting every inch of the car (this works especially well for used cars). Shake your head and laugh to yourself, look at the dealer, and raise an eyebrow. Then sigh and state, "I'll tell you what I'll do. I'll offer you ___ dollars. You should be grateful I'm willing to offer even that." When the dealer protests, say, "Fine," and walk away. See how fast they run after you!

Nowadays it seems that the cliché "It's not what you know, it's who you know" is more relevant than ever. Having friends in high places (or friends with friends in high places, or just friends in places) is the best way to get where you want to be. Networking is an essential skill, whether it puts your resume ahead of the hundreds of other applications and onto the hiring manager's desk or helps you score a beneficial deal for your small business. Learning how to work a room and follow up with contacts will bring you optimum business success.

How to Network

Following are some tips for networking that will help you stand out, increase your contacts, and get what you want.

Become visible in your field by joining professional organizations. You can make great contacts and increase your visibility by getting involved with local and national organizations. Join every group you can find that's associated with your profession. Volunteer to organize events, speak at conferences, or write articles for the association's newsletter. Do whatever it takes to get your name out there.

Don't be afraid to strike up a conversation anywhere, with anyone. A born networker loves to chat with people and doesn't limit her exchanges to organized business mixers and conferences. You can find contacts in unlikely places—on a plane ride, in line at the DMV, at your best friend's wedding, and so on. Of course, it isn't always appropriate to work the room. A wedding is one thing; a funeral is quite another. When attending a mixer, you can feel comfortable breaking the ice. Everyone is there for the same reason and no one will find it strange if you introduce yourself or join in on a group conversation with people you haven't met before. However, make sure you read your audience before you launch into a list of your professional qualifications. Depending on the type of event, people may be there just to have fun, so adjust your networking style to suit the occasion. You may be able to communicate your aptitude and skills in a more subtle way than by reading your resume.

Brush up on your small talk. Listen actively when people are talking to you and respond warmly and with interest. Wait for a fitting time to talk about yourself. When working the room, you want to be pleasant, make contact, hand over a business card if appropriate, and move on. Unless you are on to the deal of the

century or have just met a manager at your dream company (and that manager seems genuinely interested in conversing with you), you shouldn't spend too long talking to any one person. Have several polite exit lines at the ready, such as "It was lovely talking with you. Please take my card. I would love to stay in touch." Then move on to the next player.

Keep business cards with you at all times. Even if you are out of work or in school, you can develop a professional-looking card that states how to get in touch with you.

Follow up on all contacts. Simply collecting business cards doesn't count as networking. You need to follow up with all of the people you meet. To help you remember each contact you make, make notes on the back of each person's business card after you talk with her (don't do this in front of her). Send an e-mail the next day to express how much you enjoyed meeting that person. Try to be specific about where and when you met, and refer to your conversation. If you made a particularly strong or useful contact, ask her out to lunch or coffee. Don't dismiss someone just because she doesn't have exactly what you are looking for.

Be sincere. No one likes the feeling of talking to someone who is constantly scanning the room for better prospects. In today's casual business world it can be hard to tell who the most important person in the room is. The guy in the flip-flops may well be a prominent CEO, or the prominent CEO's nanny. Treat everyone well, and you will develop a Rolodex to die for.

I Can ... Negotiate!

Negotiation is a key skill when it comes to getting ahead. We are constantly negotiating, not just over raises and car deals, but also work duties, household chores, the release of hostages, and countless other daily matters. Becoming a shrewd negotiator could earn you hundreds of thousands of dollars over your lifetime, but many women are still mortified at the thought of challenging an offer and holding out for something better.

Negotiating for Success

Negotiating basically means the back-and-forth between two parties with different wants and goals who are trying to reach an agreement. In our society, women are not supposed to negotiate; we are expected to accept what we are given and not cause trouble. People hold on to these assumptions about women and use them against us in negotiations. Well, surprise—those days are over. It's time to get tough. Here's how to do it.

Get tough, get smart, and get paid. You need to assign an appropriate value to your time, your skills, and your money. Do some benchmarking to find out what others get paid for the service you provide, or what others are paying for the type of item you want to purchase. Then hold out for a price that's equivalent or better than the average.

Recognize what's negotiable and evaluate your own power. In the workplace, almost everything is negotiable. You are in a position to negotiate if someone else wants something you have—you just have to gauge what they are willing to pay for it. If your boss asks you to take on a big project, it's likely because she thinks you are the best person for the job, in which case you could negotiate for increased staff, a temporary stipend, or an early performance review. The possibilities are endless. The point here is that you need to realize what you have and what it's worth.

Plan your attack. Once you know what you want, and what you believe it's worth, you can start planning your attack. Be ready to ask for more (even substantially more) than you think you will get, and then figure out what you can be flexible about in order to reach your goal. You should also decide on your deal breaker, or absolute bottom line—at what point will you walk?

Negotiating is a two-way street. Of course, your goal is to get what you want, but if you can frame the situation so that both sides benefit, then you are more likely to prevail. Many experts talk about the "salami" technique. This basically means acquiring things in small increments instead of trying to go for the whole salami in one bite. You may not get exactly what you want, so have several alternatives in mind that you would be happy with.

Give your opponent room to negotiate. Negotiating is not the same as arguing; you are not out to prove someone else wrong, nor are negotiations always confrontational. The goal is for both sides to walk away feeling reasonably, if not completely, satisfied. If you give your opponent no room to negotiate, she is likely to shut down and give you nothing. For example, starting out by saying, "If I don't get this project assigned to me, I quit" will put you and your boss in a difficult position because you have left no room for other options. By all means, state that you want the assignment, but wait for the response before pulling out threats. Walking away or quitting should be your last card; only use it if you have exhausted all other options.

Be comfortable with winning. Women are often told that we accept defeat too easily, but we can also be poor at winning. Upon getting what we want, many women instantly feel guilty about their success, viewing it as another person's failure. We feel badly for the other party and start backtracking for fear that we have hurt the other person's feelings or created an enemy. If you have negotiated fair and square, and you have come out on top, then you have no reason for regrets. You are dealing with an equal, not a child, even if your opponent acts like one. No amount of pouting, tantrum throwing, or sullenness should affect how you feel about your deal. Just tell yourself that he should have learned to negotiate better.

Faking It!

Try applying the "free ice in winter" philosophy. Think of several things that you can offer that really won't affect you much. For example, if your personal circumstances have changed and you no longer need to work from home on Fridays, offer to give up that perk in your negotiations (without disclosing that you don't need it anymore, of course).

Men often seem to have cast-iron resistance to criticism and insults. In many male-dominated professions, such as investment banking, guys seem to thrive on being yelled at and told to improve their work—it brings out their competitive spirit and spurs them on to do better. Women, on the other hand, often shut down in the face of criticism, especially if it is delivered in a harsh or abrasive manner. Developing a thick skin in the workplace will save you a lot of heartache, and the ability to not take things personally will also make you a more productive employee.

First, you have to identify the situations in which you are taking things personally. If you are feeling slighted, insulted, blamed, or disliked, then you are probably taking things personally. This kind of reaction usually stems from a perception that we are being rejected, sidelined, or humiliated. It could also come from the feeling that we're unworthy of our position in the first place, otherwise known as "fraud syndrome."

Why Your Colleagues Make You Feel Terrible

- They don't realize you are taking it personally. Some people are just very blunt. Your boss doesn't react that way, so she assumes that nobody else does either, or she doesn't care if they do.

- They have a personal issue that they are taking out on you. This may be a need to enhance their own ego by humiliating others, or a short temper and a tendency to overreact in most situations.

- They realize you are taking things personally and are using your vulnerability to manipulate you into doing things for them or to make you look bad in front of others.

How to Handle It ·················

You cannot change the personalities of these people, but you can learn how to deal with them effectively without upsetting yourself in the process. Follow these tips the next time you start to react emotionally in your workplace:

- In the case of the blunt boss, try to look at her point objectively and evaluate its validity. Did your report suck as much as she said it did? If you can't come up with a reasonable explanation, meet with her to discuss her expectations (for tips, see "I Can . . . Get to the Point!" page 86).

- Remember that what you do does not and should not define who you are. Someone who challenges your work or your opinion is not challenging you as a human being.

- Stick to your guns. Just like the schoolyard, the office often has its own bully. Don't let someone sideline you by being louder or ruder.

- Stay calm. Don't give the egomaniac in the cube next to yours the pleasure of seeing you flustered.

- Your critic is only offering his personal opinion. What he thinks is not the truth; it's just one interpretation of the situation. It is okay to disagree.

- Don't escalate an unpleasant situation. Remaining professional at all times is one of the best ways to not take it personally. This is also a fun tactic, since it frustrates yellers to no end.

- Some coworkers and supervisors are simply toxic people. If their bad behavior is completely unreasonable and is affecting your work, talk to your human resources department about filing a complaint for harassment.

We can all learn something from coworkers who let insults slide right off of them like water off a duck's back. Stick to the facts and try not to let emotion or anger cloud your judgment. The sooner you can stop taking it personally, the happier you will be. It's just work, after all.

EXTRA CREDIT!

Ever heard the maxim "Don't wrestle with a pig; you'll both get covered in mud and the pig loves it"? Identify the "pigs" in your work world and make a list of times they have managed to get you covered in mud. Once you know how they push your buttons, you can devise strategies to avoid taking their crap personally in those circumstances.

I Can ... Brag!

Contrary to what your mother may have told you, bragging isn't always a crime. The ability to highlight your achievements in a non-offensive manner is easy to develop and, when done correctly, will sound absolutely nothing like showing off.

Why Brag?

Because no one else will do it for you. It is a mistake to think that your boss and coworkers automatically notice how good you are at your job, or that they realize how many improvements you have made to your department. It's not enough to be an outstanding employee—people need to *know* that you are an outstanding employee, and one way they are going to know is if you find a way to tell them.

Toot Your Own Horn

No one wants to be thought of as a braggart. We were raised to be humble,

which is certainly an admirable trait. But if you find yourself constantly overlooked or passed over for promotion while show-off Shelley wins praise and bonuses for doing almost nothing, then you need to learn how to brag. Just a little bit. Here are some tips for bragging without boasting:

- Become involved with high-profile work projects that are vital to the company. If you are involved with projects that are highly visible, you will have more opportunities to discuss your successes.

- Lose the self-deprecating humor. Never put yourself down in front of others, even if you think you are merely being modest.

- If a customer or client is pleased with your work, ask him or her to write or e-mail your supervisor. The client will usually be more than happy to pass along a rave review of your performance.

- An easy way to brag is to get others to do it for you. Compliment others frequently, because it will make them more likely to compliment you. Don't reserve your compliments for supervisors and managers (that's just kissing up). Instead, be equally supportive of everyone in the organization, creating a positive buzz around your professional image.

- If you get a great result on a project or deal, send an e-mail or memo to your boss highlighting the good news. Be sure to praise everyone involved, using "we" instead of "I"—you will still receive more of the credit if the e-mail comes from you. Do use this tactic sparingly, though, reserving it for true triumphs.

- Keep a "brag" folder containing e-mails and letters of praise that you have received. Include your own notes and documentation detailing your achievements throughout the year. You can pull out this folder when your annual review comes around, or flip through it to boost your spirits when you are having a bad day.

But Don't Blow it! ················

Nobody likes a person who constantly talks about how great she is. It impresses only the most gullible of listeners, and it leads everyone else to roll their eyes and plot the braggart's downfall. To prevent your bragging from seriously backfiring, keep the following in mind:

- Don't take credit for other people's work or ideas. Giving credit where credit is due will do much more to improve your image than getting a reputation as a parasite.

- Stick to the facts. Never embellish your accomplishments or make statements that will later prove to be false.

- Make sure you brag at the right moments. If your company has just lost a major client, now might not be the best time to point out that your end of the project was flawless.

- Never talk about how much money you earn, how big your raise was, or how much your house cost. Discussing your personal finances is just plain tasteless. There are many subtler ways to demonstrate your wealth, if that's what matters to you.

- Don't brag by comparing yourself favorably to others. It is one thing to say "I was really pleased with the $20,000 deal I just closed." It is entirely different to proclaim, "I just closed a $20,000 deal. That's $10,000 more than Jane did in the whole of last month!"

I Can... Argue!

The ability to argue your point is as important in the workplace as it is in your personal relationships. All too often we fail to stick to our guns in a disagreement with coworkers, even when we truly believe we are in the right. The good news is that, even if you think confrontation is the scariest thing since headcheese, you can learn how to argue effectively.

Arguing: Basic Level

Arguing in the workplace isn't something you want to use as your usual form of communication. You don't want to get a reputation as an unhinged lunatic who will yell and scream at a moment's notice. The aim is to be able to defend your ideas and not be railroaded by more aggressive colleagues in front of your boss.

- Only enter into an argument if you genuinely believe in the point you are making and think that your company or project will benefit if others see it your way.

- Pick your battles. You can't argue everything.

- Be prepared to back your argument up with details and data. You must be able to clearly articulate why you think you are in the right.

- Remain calm, regardless of how your challenger is behaving. State your point firmly and consistently.

- Keep the focus on resolving the issue, not triumphing over your coworker, and avoid being defensive. Your ideas are being challenged, not you.

- Similarly, never resort to personal insults or slams—challenge ideas, not individuals. You have to work with these people!

- Genuinely try to listen to the other side. You may come to realize that you and your challenger are not as far from agreement as you think.

- Avoid arguing with idiots. There is no point in engaging with someone who won't listen to you or allow you the opportunity to speak.

- Be prepared to exit the argument. If it's getting out of hand, say, "I think we have spent enough time on this. Let's continue this conversation after the meeting."

- Accept losses gracefully. If you have listened to the other side and been proven wrong, say so and move on.

Arguing: Master's Level · · · · · · · ·

Master's-level arguing usually involves disagreeing with your boss or other high-ranking folk. While many of the above points are still applicable, you should also keep the following in mind:

- Try not to challenge your boss in front of others, except to prevent serious, unpleasant consequences.

- Think of arguments with your boss as efforts to steer her toward the right course of action and to warn her of mistakes or pitfalls you may be anticipating.

- Always have your facts straight. Be prepared to state the problem as you see it, offer a solution, and provide details to back it up.

- Listen to what your boss has to say, repeat what you think she has said, and then ask permission to add a thought or idea. This approach will allow you to avoid openly disagreeing with her.

- Don't go behind your boss's back and tell other colleagues that you disagree with her, and don't go over her head unless you have no other options.

Arguing: Drunken Level · · · · · · · ·

Drunken-level arguing is the most common, the most fun, and the most dangerous. This is unlikely to happen during work hours (unless you have a drinking problem), but when you're at a party or other social event here's how to do it:

- The louder you are, the more correct you are.

- Facts are not necessary; they only complicate your brilliant argument.

- If facts are required, feel free to make them up, especially statistics. It is practically impossible to argue with someone who is making up numbers.

- Personal insults are welcome and encouraged.

- If you're really drunk, the best way to end an argument (regardless of the topic) is to start crying and tell your opponent first that you love her and then that you hate her, in rapid succession.

- The whole point is to be right and to make others feel stupid. You should stop at nothing to achieve this.

Faking It!

If you are feeling attacked or backed into a corner, attempt to turn the tables on your challenger. Instead of defending your position, start attacking his or her points and demanding facts to back them up. Expert arguers all share this skill—they can discredit someone else's opinion without ever really voicing one of their own.

I Can ... Razz!

Also known as "joshing," "kidding," "ragging," and "ribbing," *razzing* is a form of teasing peculiar to groups of young men, which allows guys to pick on and humiliate each other, all in the name of good old-fashioned fun! Most often they leave the ladies out of their good-humored banter (perhaps because, for some reason, we don't find jokes about our mothers amusing), but if you want to dish it out to the guys you need to learn how to razz.

Razzing is relatively mild in nature, such as teasing someone who misses an easy shot in a game or turns up at the office with a hickey. It should not stray into the realm of bullying and, if it's done in the workplace, it must not touch on sensitive issues like gender, ethnicity, height, weight, sexuality, and religion. That would be harassment, not razzing, and would land you in a world of trouble.

Razz-amatazz Rules

Following are the guidelines for effective and brilliant razzing.

- For some reason, it seems appropriate to call people only by their last names

when razzing, as in "Hey, Walsh, 1980 called. It wants its pants back."

- You have to be quick on the draw. Being the first to razz someone is much cooler than joining in on an already established razz.

- Razzing the razzer can also be a classy move. If some of your coworkers start ganging up on the guy with the Celine Dion T-shirt, don't join in. Instead, turn the tables on the ringleader: "Whatever, Karsh. It's better than that Phil Collins hairdo you've got going on."

- Stick to safe razzing topics. You are not setting out to land someone in therapy. Making fun of a crazy haircut or teasing someone for being in love is usually acceptable. Telling the office computer geek that he can't get a date because he is an ugly troll with the breath of a warthog? Not so acceptable.

- On the other hand, if your razz is directed at someone with the ego of an NBA player, or if it's blatantly not true, you can get away with a lot more. If you tell the office hottie that he can't get a date because he's an ugly troll with the breath of a warthog, you will probably not damage him too much.

- If you dish it out, you have to be able to take it. Period.

Faking It!

One of the easiest ways to razz someone is to recite lines from key guy films. Think *Animal House*, not *Pretty in Pink*.

"hey Smith, °°° nice mullet"

Do you ever find that you are telling your boyfriend, husband, or other male person a fascinating story about what happened to your friend Kate on the bus the other day, only to realize that he is not listening? Turns out that the level of conversational detail we find necessary is a lot higher than our male counterparts are capable of listening to.

In the office, getting to the point quickly and succinctly is a vital communication skill. Padding your statements with all kinds of extraneous information will only weaken your point. Including every detail of Ted and Kathy's breakup is probably still essential if you are talking to your best friend, but relaying every detail of your conversation with the copier salesman to anyone is just plain boring.

Cut to the Chase

Not sure whether you're a rambler? You have trouble getting to the point if any of the following are true:

- People often interrupt you.

- People finish your stories or sentences for you.

- People start fidgeting and their eyes glaze over when you start talking.

In business, we encounter many situations in which we have a short time to make an impression, such as in an e-mail, in a proposal, or during a client meeting. If we don't grab listeners' attention in the first few seconds, we may lose a crucial opportunity to get our point across. So skip the boring preamble and cut to the chase.

- Avoid all details that are not directly related to your point. If it doesn't matter that the events you're describing happened last Tuesday, don't mention it.

- Cut out unnecessary and tangential anecdotes. Save your funny, shocking, or embarrassing stories for another time.

- Don't recite dialogue. Telling everyone what you said, what Jim said, what you replied, what Jim said back to you is unnecessary and time consuming.

- Say it only once, using as few words as possible. Unless you're asked to clarify or repeat something, avoid restating the same thing, even if you think you are saying it in a different way.

- Avoid using space fillers such as "um," "ah," and "you know?" Not only do they take up time, but they also make you sound inarticulate and unsure of yourself.

- When in a meeting, only ask questions that are relevant to the discussion and to the style or purpose of the meeting. If you are planning a conference a year ahead of time, asking questions about the sandwiches or the timing of specific events will only bog things down and drive people nuts. Similarly, asking questions that are relevant only to you is useless and annoying. Don't ask questions merely to validate your presence.

Remember, you can't expect others to see your point if you never reach it. Get rid of the filler and you will have a much easier time making yourself understood.

EXTRA CREDIT!

Take a complicated story or situation and practice explaining it in one minute or less. This will force you to recognize the key points and focus on them alone.

Are You a Mogul or a Mouse?

1. Before purchasing a car, you should determine

   a. The invoice price

   b. The MSRP

   c. The MSG

2. When bragging, you should never

   a. Talk about your personal finances

   b. Talk about your personal life

   c. Talk about your sex life

3. If you have trouble getting to the point:

   a. Practice telling a story in one minute or less.

   b. Practice telling a story in ten minutes or less.

   c. Practice telling a story to everyone you know.

4. When razzing, you should

   a. Call people by their last names

   b. Call people by their nicknames

   c. Call someone a moron

5. One common mistake women make when negotiating is

   a. Feeling guilty about getting what they want

   b. Asking for too much

   c. Asking the boss out on a date

Mostly *A*'s: Upwardly mobile!

Martha Stewart in the making! You have developed the skills to get ahead in the business world without being a total jerk. Keep up the good work and storm your way to the top!

Mostly *B*'s: Upwardly stable!

You are probably doing pretty well for yourself, but something is holding you back. Focus on what you want, and don't be afraid to ask for what you deserve.

Mostly *C*'s: Downward spiral!

For some reason, you just can't kick-start your career. Are you too busy having fun, perhaps?

Home Improvement

When Annie Lennox and Aretha Franklin sang "Sisters Are Doing It for Themselves," little did they know that they were creating an anthem for an army of female do-it-yourselfers. With the number of female homeowners doubling in the last few years, there is no doubt about it—the modern handywoman is doing it for herself, all around the house.

The concept that began with *This Old House* has undergone a serious makeover—it seems you can't turn on the television without seeing a blonde bombshell in a tool belt who's up to her eyeballs in spackle. Mysteriously, home improvement has managed to become almost sexy, and millions of viewers tune in every day to see how they too can create a French colonial bedroom for less than $100. Suddenly, we are not just obsessed with the results; we are obsessed with creating the results ourselves.

Women are flooding hardware stores, taking classes, and snatching up the new array of tools that are emerging just for them. While the pink power drill has not proved particularly popular (we hear Barbie has one), manufacturers are spending some serious cash to tap the female market.

This chapter covers some of the basics of home repair, but it also delves into a range of skills that were previously reserved for men. From unclogging the toilet to putting up shelves, and carving a Thanksgiving turkey, we will teach you how to rule your roost with ease.

Owning these skills is essential for the woman living alone or for the woman who is tired of waiting for her man to turn off the golf and turn his attention to mowing the lawn. But be warned! You may already be doing more than your fair share in the home, so if you take on handywoman duties on top of everything else, be sure to trade out some less exciting chores (kitchen floors? dusting?) to keep things equal.

Now grab your hammer, tighten your tool belt, and get ready for some serious DIY!

This useful yet disgusting skill is unfortunately a must-have. There is nothing worse than flushing the toilet and watching in horror as the water (along with its contents) starts rapidly rising toward the top of the bowl. A dependable toilet makes life that much easier. However, if you live in an old building, or one that has suffered a cheap bathroom remodel, you may find that your throne has a few quirks. You can always call the experts, but waiting two hours for a close-up view of the plumber's crack is about as appealing as doing the job yourself, and you have to pay serious money for the privilege. So you might as well tackle it on your own for free!

A Clog in the Bog

Toilets overflow because they are clogged. If the clog is not too serious, you should be able to take care of it yourself. In order to find out how serious it is, make sure that the clog really is in the toilet. If water is coming up out of your sink or bathtub drain, then the clog is farther down the pipeline and not so easy to fix. If water is rising through other drains in the house, then it is probably a sewer issue, which, we are afraid, is beyond our skill set.

Simple clogs (those caused by waste and not by objects accidentally flushed down the toilet) can most often be fixed with a plunger. Pop for a high-quality plunger;

you will be thankful later. There are two types of plunger—the old-fashioned cup style, and the more modern flange style, which looks like an accordion on a stick. Both are effective, but the flange plunger is probably easier to use and gives better results.

Plunge and Expunge · · · · · · · · · · · ·

If the bowl is empty, pour water into it until it is half full. However, if the bowl is close to overflowing, you may want to remove some of the water before plunging. Place the plunger into the toilet, completely covering the drain opening. Press down firmly on the plunger and release. Do this for fifteen to twenty seconds, keeping the drain hole firmly covered. If the water level starts to go down, add more water and repeat. If the water looks like it is draining normally, try flushing. If it works properly, the clog has been cleared. If not, you need to move on to more serious equipment: the drain snake (yikes!).

A drain snake is a spiral of wire, connected to a flexible wire that can navigate the pipes in the toilet. It will also have a hand crank and a guide tube. Insert the guide tube into the bowl with the curve facing the direction of the drain. Crank the handle until it becomes tight, and then crank in the opposite direction. Repeat until it has gone in as far as it will go (get your mind out of the sewer!). Pull the guide tube out of the toilet, pushing and pulling gently. If it gets stuck, don't force it, or you may break your toilet bowl. Repeat the plunging process described above, and then try flushing.

If none of these techniques work, then you have a serious drainage problem. Give in and call a plumber for help.

Random Fact: The average person will spend three years on the toilet during his or her life. We visit the toilet well over two thousand times each year. No wonder it gets clogged!

Hanging a picture, photograph, or framed mirror is one of the quickest and easiest ways to decorate your home. But if you are anything like us—the old us, that is—a sudden urge to brighten your walls by hanging a few framed pictures most often results in walls so full of holes that they look like Swiss cheese. While we agree that all home improvement projects should be attempted with gusto, it might be worth following a few simple instructions before you get out the hammer and nails and start breaking down the drywall.

How to Hang

Follow these easy steps for stylish picture hanging:

1. The first step is to figure out where to hang it. Most people tend to hang pictures too high on the wall, or choose a frame that is too small for the space. A good rule of thumb is to hang your picture so the top of the frame is at eye level (around 5 feet 8 inches). However, if the picture will hang in an area used mainly for seating, then you should hang it lower; if it is in an area used only for standing, like a foyer or hallway, then hang it slightly higher.

2. Wall art should be used to extend the lines of your room, making it appear more spacious. If your piece is too small, try grouping it with other pieces of a similar type—pictures with the same theme, same colors, or other common element.

Arrange the pieces on the floor near the wall on which you intend to hang them in order to get a clear idea of how they'll look once they're on your wall. You will also want to consider how elements like direct sunlight and moisture will affect your artwork, and avoid these as necessary.

3. The next step is to decide what equipment you will need. For this, you need to know two things: the weight of the picture and whether you will be mounting it to a wall stud or drywall. When you buy picture hooks, it is important to check the package to see how much weight each will hold. (Do use picture hooks, because nails alone will bend easily and could send your artwork crashing to the floor.) Hooks are usually available in three sizes; the 20- and 30-pound hangers require only one nail, and the 40-pound hanger requires two.

Some people will say that you must hang heavy items from a wall stud or beam. You can use a device called a "stud detector" for this purpose—for finding the wall stud, not for finding you a date. You can also use the old-fashioned method of tapping the wall until the sound changes from hollow to dull. The dull sound means you've found a wall stud (these are usually equidistant from each other, around 16 inches apart). A good trick is to find an outlet or a light switch, which usually has a stud immediately to one side of it, so you can generally start measuring 16-inch intervals from there to find a stud in the right place.

However, the lack of a stud in the perfect place in your wall does not mean that you cannot hang your piece. It just means that you will need some special equipment—a toggle bolt or a molly bolt, which is basically a screw with wings that expand once they are screwed into the wall. Toggle or molly bolts are only necessary for extremely heavy pieces, and your local hardware store should be able to help you determine if you'll need one. A regular picture hook and nail is just fine for many frames, with or without a wall stud.

4. Now that you are ready to hang the picture, hold it to the wall and make a small mark where the top of the frame will be. Next, hold the wire behind the picture taut and measure from the wire to the frame's top edge. Measure down from your original mark on the wall and make another mark—this is where your picture hook will go. The same method works for frames with a hanging tab; just measure from the tab to the top of the frame. To avoid cracking the surrounding paint, place a piece of masking (not Scotch) tape where the nail will go. Finally, nail the hook into the wall where you made your second mark, hang your picture, and adjust it so it's straight.

Follow these simple instructions and your home will look like a glamorous art gallery in no time—just not a gallery filled with framed David Hasselhoff photos, we hope.

Faking It!

You can use pictures and wall hangings to change the atmosphere of your room. In a small room, try using pictures that give a horizontal impression, such as panoramic images of a beach or landscape, to create the illusion of width. In a room with a low ceiling, use vertical-themed pictures of trees or tall buildings to add a feeling of height.

I Can... Put Up Shelves!

Putting up shelves is tricky and mired with pitfalls. If you don't take certain precautionary steps, you will end up with a lopsided mess that will come crashing down as soon you put so much as a teacup on it. The good news is that this job involves power tools, in the form of the handy electric drill. Every aspiring do-it-yourselfer should have one of these in her tool belt.

Perfect Placement

To put up shelves properly, follow the steps below:

1. Before you do anything, decide where you are going to put your shelves.

2. This project will involve using an electric drill, and you'll need to make sure that you will not drill into any pipes or electrical wires. Use a pipe and cable detector (available at hardware stores) to check.

3. Shelves that will only hold very light objects can be attached to the wall with drywall anchors and screws or toggle bolts (see "I Can . . . Hang a Picture!" page 94), but anything designed to hold heavier objects must be set on brackets, which will need to be screwed into the wall studs. Use a stud detector (see page 95), or tap the wall and listen to find the studs (a hollow sound means drywall; a dull sound means you've found a wall stud). Wall studs are evenly spaced at around 16 inches apart.

4. Always remember the DIY adage: "Measure twice, drill once." With this in

mind, mark the spot on the wall where you want the shelves to go, and then use a spirit level (a tool that uses an air bubble encased in liquid to help you determine if things such as shelves are level) to line up where the brackets will go (spaced about every 24 inches). Mark the spots with a pencil. If you don't have a level, measure down from two or more spots on the ceiling with a tape measure to make sure your markings are even. The longer your shelf and the heavier the objects placed on it, the more brackets you will need. Once you are sure your

markings are the right distance apart, evenly spaced, and level to each other, you can begin drilling.

5. Select the drill bit that matches the size of your drywall anchors. (Also known as a "wall plug," a drywall anchor is a plastic plug inserted into the drilled hole. The screw is then screwed into the wall plug, so the wall plug should match the size of the screw on the inside, and the size of the drilled hole on the outside. You will not need to use drywall anchors if attaching your shelves to a

wall stud.) Use tape to mark the depth of the drywall anchor on the drill bit so you know when to stop drilling. Drill all of the screw holes into the wall to the depth of the anchors. Make sure you are using screws that are at least an inch long in order to properly secure the brackets to the walls.

6. Once you have inserted the drywall anchors into the drilled holes, screw the brackets to the wall using a screwdriver or the screwdriver attachment of your drill. Put the shelf (painted or varnished and dried first, of course) on top of the brackets and attach the shelf using screws or panel pins to prevent them from tipping forward when a heavy object is placed on them.

Don't you just love power tools?

I Can... Open a Jar!

All you want to do is consume as many pickles as is humanly possible in a short period of time. But the lid is stuck. It just won't budge, forcing you to humbly approach the nearest man creature and ask him to do it for you, which he often (but not always) does with irritating ease. You must have loosened it for him, right? Well, just as we have used science to help men overcome some of their inadequacies, we must now apply scientific principles to the opening of a jar of pickles.

There are many products available now that will do this job for you mechanically, but most are really just fancy variations on good old-fashioned home fixes. So save yourself $50 by trying the following simple tricks.

Jar-opening problems come in two main categories: an unbreakable seal and lack of a decent grip. Overcome these hurdles and you will never have to contemplate smashing a jar with a hammer again.

Break the Seal

Here are several tips that you can try when faced with a jar with an unbreakable seal.

- Turn the jar upside down and hit the bottom several times with the heel of your hand to break the seal. Or, you can hit around the circumference of the jar lid with the end of a wooden spoon, handle of a butter knife, or similar blunt, heavy object.

- Insert the blade of a sturdy butter knife under the edge of the lid. Do this several times in different places around the top of the jar until you hear a pop. You should now be able to open the jar with ease.

- If the lid of the jar is made of metal, run it under hot water from the tap in order to expand the metal and loosen the lid.

- If you won't need to reseal the jar after you use it, puncture the lid with a sharp object to break the seal.

- When resealing the jar, rub a few drops of oil around the edge to avoid a similar problem in the future.

Get a Grip ·······················

When you're in the throes of a gripping problem, try any of these tricks.

- Wrap a thick rubber band around the jar lid for extra grip.

- Use a latex or rubber glove to increase your grip on the lid, then twist.

- Instead of holding the jar away from you, hold it close to your body and try to turn the jar and not the lid.

Now, you can show up the boys the next time they fail in this manly task!

EXTRA CREDIT!

A good grip is essential to the ability to open jars. You can improve your grip by repeatedly squeezing a tennis ball for six seconds and then releasing. You can also purchase a hand gripper from a sporting goods store and work out your grip that way. Do this exercise several times a week.

I Can... Carve Meat!

Perhaps it's the knife sharpening, or the artistry, or just a love of big slabs of cooked meat—whatever the reason, men love to carve. We are not suggesting that you take this task away from them (most do too little around the house as it is), but should you find yourself at the Thanksgiving table with no suitably trained knife-wielding man on hand, you'll be glad we didn't leave you in the lurch.

Carving Basics

A few general principles apply to carving, regardless of the type or cut of meat:

- A decent carving knife is essential, and it needs to be sharp.

- The meat should be properly cooked—overdone or underdone meat is much harder to carve.

- Before you carve, leave the meat to "rest" on a cutting board for 15 minutes after you take it out of the oven. This allows the juices to redistribute.

- Have a warm platter nearby on which to serve the meat.

- If you are anticipating leftovers, don't carve all of the meat. Sliced meat dries out faster than a solid piece.

- Avoid piercing the meat too many times with a fork, since this will release the juices.

- When slicing beef, lamb, and pork, carve against the grain for the most

tender cut (if the grain is running up and down, cut across).

• Start cutting with a gentle sawing motion. Once you have started cutting, continue until the slice is complete.

Chicken and Turkey · · · · · · · · · · · · ·

1. Start carving the side closest to you. Pull the leg away from the bird as the knife separates it from the body. Remove the leg and then cut the slices of darker meat from the thigh and drumstick.

2. Hold the bird steady with a large fork and start carving the breast downward toward the cutting board or plate, beginning partway down and using long, even strokes. Slices should be about ¼ inch thick.

3. For each new slice, move higher up the breast until you reach the top of the breastbone, moving each slice to your warmed platter.

4. Repeat on the other side of the bird.

Beef, Pork, and Lamb · · · · · · · · · · ·

Place the roast so the widest side is to your right (place it toward the left if you're left-handed).

- Cut thin slices (thick enough to be slices, not shavings). However, if your meat is a tender cut, then you'll want to cut thicker slices to prevent them from falling apart.

- For a rump roast of beef, start cutting at the small end if you are planning to have leftovers. If not, you can carve lengthwise instead for bigger slices. Slices should be no more than ¼ inch thick.

- For ham, carve as you would a rump roast (smallest end first), slicing almost to the bone. Slices should be very thin.

If you buy your meat from a reputable butcher, he or she should be able to give you guidance about the correct cut and method of carving. Carving meat is harder than you might think, so remember to save the best slices for yourself as a reward for your hard work.

The Jargon

Chuck: A cut from the shoulder and neck of the beef; should be stewed for best results

Rib: A tender and excellent cut for roasting (as in "prime rib") or for steaks

Loin: The tastiest part of the beef, yielding the tenderloin (filet mignon), sirloin, and top loin

Rump roast: A cut from the rear end of the beef; best used for pot roast

---

I Can... Flip an Egg!

There are a few kitchen-specific skills at which men believe they excel. Unfortunately, none of these involve cleaning the refrigerator or kitchen floor—but we digress. Egg flipping without breaking the yolk, which does involve a certain amount of talent, falls into this category. Follow these simple instructions the next time a fried-egg sandwich craving is upon you.

Crack It

1. In a heavy frying pan, heat a tablespoon of oil over high heat. For extra yumminess, use the fat left over from frying bacon. If you are a girlie-girl, or a vegetarian, use a light oil such as canola. If you use butter instead, you will have to use lower heat to prevent it from burning.

2. When the fat is hot, crack the egg low over the pan, letting the egg slide in carefully to avoid breaking the yolk.

3. Cook over high heat for 30 seconds, and then jiggle the pan to make sure the egg is not sticking. Keep cooking on high for another 30 seconds, then lower the heat to medium and cook until the whites set and become opaque.

4. If you are a sunny-side-up fan, this should give you a perfect egg—slightly crispy on the outside, with a firm white and a runny yolk. Slide the egg onto the plate or slice of toast and enjoy. If you are an over-easy, over-medium, or over-hard fan, get ready for the egg flip.

5. When the white becomes opaque, jiggle the pan again to make sure the egg is ready to flip.

6. Lift the pan about a foot above the heat. With a good grip on the handle, jerk the pan away from you and then snap it back, causing the egg to jump out of the pan and rotate in the air.

7. Bring the pan up to catch the egg. The less distance it travels, the less likely you are to break the yolk.

8. Cook for another 30 seconds or so, depending on your preference, and then repeat the flip.

9. Slide the egg onto the plate or bread and enjoy.

You can also use a spatula to flip the egg, but this is much less impressive. The first few times you try this technique, you will probably break the yolk. If so, just act like you meant to do it until you perfect the art. Before long you will be flipping like a pro.

The Jargon

Sunny-side up: An egg fried on only one side so the yolk remains uncooked

Over easy: An egg fried on one side and then flipped over and fried briefly on the other side

Over medium: Like over easy, but cooked for longer on the flip side so the yolk becomes firmer

Over hard: Like over easy and over medium, but cooked long enough on the flip side for the yolk to become solid

I Can... Lift Heavy Objects!

Men, like other beasts of burden, are naturally stronger than women and for this reason alone the majority of heavy lifting should be left to them. However, sometimes a girl has to carry her IKEA dresser up four flights of stairs all by herself. And, yes, there is a way to do this without landing yourself in the emergency room with a slipped disk.

Rules to Lift By

Follow these rules to avoid serious injury:

- Use the major muscles in your legs and your butt, not your back, to lift heavy objects.

- Always bend your knees and keep your back vertical. Bending forward will put extra strain on your lower back.

- Stand close to the object you are trying to lift, no more than 8 inches away. The farther away you are, the less able you will be to employ your leg muscles.

- Avoid lifting objects above chest level.

- Avoid twisting when lifting or carrying heavy objects.

- Fatigued muscles are more prone to injury. Take frequent breaks while lifting. Extremely heavy objects should not be lifted without help or machinery.

Lifting Do's and Don'ts ··········

- **Do** keep your feet shoulder-width, or even farther, apart.

- **Don't** carry a load that is unbalanced, such as a box that is heavier on one side than the other.

- **Don't** go immediately from sitting to lifting heavy objects; do a few stretches first to prepare your back and leg muscles.

- **Do** use both hands, with the weight equally distributed.

- **Don't** attempt to lift objects that are too heavy for you.

- **Do** suck it up and call on a stronger friend or neighbor when you need help. Wounded pride heals much faster than a hernia.

Faking It!

Use the proper equipment to make heavy lifting a little easier. A hand truck or dolly is a great tool for shifting heavy things around. You can get a collapsible version to fit in the trunk of your car, and even special dollies to move specific items like pool tables and pinball machines.

I Can... *Fit a Sofa through a Door!*

Trying to move a sofa, large dresser or, heaven forbid, a piano through a narrow doorway can be both comical and frustrating. It is often best left to the experts, but if your moving crew consists of available friends and family, figuring out how to get the sofa through the door before you start your move will save you a lot of time and effort.

Sofa So Good

If you're hauling a truckload of furniture, plan to move the large and heavy items first while your moving team is still feeling fit and strong.

1. Measure the doorway and the couch. Don't panic if the sofa is slightly longer than the doorway is tall (it can even be significantly longer if there is a straight path into the room), or if you are trying to get around a tight corner. Do panic if your sofa is wider, at its narrowest, than your door. If you are way off in your dimensions, you will need either a new couch or a new place to live.

2. If necessary, take the door off its hinges in order to give you a few more inches.

3. Attach cardboard to your door frame to protect it and your sofa from dings, dents, and tears.

4. Remove all cushions and, if possible, the legs of the sofa.

5. Stand the couch on its end, completely upright, next to the door.

6. Have one of your helpers stand inside the door to hold the higher end and another outside to lift the lower end. The stronger person should be holding the lower end, since she will do more of the actual lifting.

7. The person inside the door should now carefully and slowly tip the sofa toward her until it's at a 45-degree angle to the floor.

8. Start moving the sofa through the door. The person with the higher end should keep it as high as possible, and the lower-end lifter should keep it as low as possible, with the sofa still at a 45-degree angle.

9. Reward your movers with copious amounts of beer and pizza.

If you follow these instructions and still don't succeed, then you could be in trouble. In extreme circumstances, a couch can be lifted through the window, or even cut into sections and joined together again. For the most part, though, with a little wiggling and jiggling and a fair amount of swearing, you should be able to manage it. Make sure you really like your new place— after all this effort you may never want to move again.

EXTRA CREDIT!

Here's how to move an upright piano. Lower and lock the lid prior to moving, and have at least one person on each end. Move the piano slowly, a few inches at a time, onto a heavy-duty four-wheel dolly. Wheel the piano slowly to avoid tipping it over. But the real key is this: Before you start, make sure you have more than enough people on hand; this will make this difficult task as easy as possible.

I Can... Mow the Lawn!

Lawn maintenance is big business (read: expensive) these days, but you can save yourself some cash by learning to mow your own lawn. While a perfectly manicured lawn is a joy to behold, it does take work. If your lawn is looking more like an overgrown jungle than a beautiful, springy green carpet, you need to get mowing!

What to Buy

Unless you live on a farm or a large estate (in which case you probably just pay someone to mow for you), you won't need anything more than a regular rotary mower. Go for an electric mower to avoid having to carry around cans of gasoline. You should also invest in an edger, to get that neat and tidy look along the edges of flower beds, tree trunks, and other hard-to-reach areas.

When to Mow

Different types of grass have different optimum lengths. Your grass should not be allowed to grow more than a third above its ideal length. For example, if your grass should be 2 inches in length, when it reaches 3 inches you need to get the mower out.

Don't cut your grass when it's wet (which is probably why we associate the droning sound of mowers with the first warm days of spring). You should also avoid mowing when your grass is weak, such as during a long dry spell.

How to Mow ·

Follow these tips for an impeccably manicured lawn:

• Clear your lawn of rocks and other debris before you commence mowing.

• Always move your mower forward. Only go backward if it is necessary to get out of a tight spot.

• Mow slopes by going from side to side, not up and down.

• Mow in a consistent direction during each mowing. However, the next time you mow, change the direction by 90 degrees to avoid weakening the grass.

• Never leave a running mower unattended, and keep children and animals away while mowing.

• Use an edger for tight or irregular spots, like the bases of tree trunks or tight corners.

• Allow grass trimmings to remain on your lawn as fertilizer. This practice is called "grasscycling"; because all those clippings stay in your yard instead of going into the landfill, it's good for the environment as well as your lawn. If you cut your grass regularly, the clippings will be short enough that you won't notice them.

When you're finished mowing, enjoy your fragrant, freshly cut grass by relaxing with a cool glass of wine (if you don't have hay fever, that is).

Random Fact: The early nineteenth century saw the dawn of sports played on flat, grass-covered grounds (such as soccer, cricket, and croquet), requiring an easy way of maintaining the grass. The lawn mower was invented in England in 1830 by Edwin Beard Budding, in order to meet this newly emerging need.

I Can... Kill Spiders and Insects!

The sight of a big, black, hairy spider scuttling toward your feet as you stand naked in the shower is enough to strike terror in the hearts of most women. For whatever reason, the killing of vermin and pests has remained a manly task—no man worth his machismo could ever admit to being afraid of a little creepy crawly, so when called upon for bug-swatting duties he has no choice but to comply.

It's not that men are better at wielding a shoe or a rolled-up newspaper, or that their bug-crushing aim is better than ours. Their ability to kill insects stems from the fact that they were not taught to be afraid of them. They were the ones chasing us around the school yard with worms, and not the other way around. Conquer your fears and you too can become a bold insect destroyer.

Entomophobia Be Gone!

We fear things for a reason. Fear is our brain's signal that we are in danger. If we feel fear when we see a poisonous snake, it can save our lives. A phobia, however, arises when we feel fear in situations that do not warrant it. In other words, we become afraid of all snakes, not just the dangerous ones.

If you start shaking, sweating, and feeling ill when you see even the tiniest spider, then you may have a pretty serious phobia, and there's probably not much we can do for you. But most of us fear insects simply because they are icky and ugly, they move quickly, and they might crawl on us. Here's how to handle one of these creepy critters:

- Relaxation is the opposite of anxiety. Take calming breaths and bring yourself back to reality before confronting the ugly beast.

- Keep things in perspective. The typical insect you might encounter in your house is not more than an inch long. It also doesn't have a giant shoe to hit you with, or a can of Raid to poison you with. You have the upper hand in this battle.

- Choose the right weapon. An object with some weight to it that is easy to maneuver, such as a rolled-up newspaper, is ideal.

- Try to get rid of the insect without getting too close to it. The hose on your vacuum cleaner is a great way to suck up insects, spiders, spider webs, and bug eggs while keeping yourself a good few feet away.

Buzz Kills

Some methods work better for certain insects than others. And if you are concerned about your karma or the harmful health effects of insect spray, try these alternatives:

- A carnivorous plant will take care of pesky house flies—some species can eat up to one thousand each year!

- If you don't like to kill the little critters, you can buy catch-and-release systems to trap spiders.

- The most effective way to control roaches is to cut off their source of food. Tightly cover and seal all food containers, and never leave crumbs on your counter or dishes in the sink. Pretty soon they will find a greener pasture to invade.

- In addition to killing mice, cats love to chase spiders and insects, and some are pretty good at catching them.

- Remember that having spiders in your home is considered lucky by some, foretelling wealth and good fortune. They are also useful because they catch other insects—unlike roaches, which are just plain disgusting and should be violently killed.

Random Fact: Cockroaches are hard to kill for a reason. A roach can live up to a month without food and up to a week without its head! Some poor female cockroaches are pregnant for their entire lives.

Are You a Fix-It Fanatic or a Fool with a Tool?

1. The best way to find a stud is to

    a. Tap along the wall until you hear a dull sound

    b. Use a stud detector

    c. Go to the hardware store in a bikini

2. You need to mow your lawn when

    a. The grass has grown to a third over its optimum length

    b. Your cat has been lost for three days in the overgrowth

    c. You move the rusted car on blocks to the junkyard and discover you actually have a lawn

3. To carve meat correctly you need

    a. A recently sharpened knife

    b. A recently sharpened electric knife

    c. A dull Swiss Army knife

4. To unclog your toilet, it's best to use

    a. A plunger or a drain snake in extreme cases

    b. A plumber in extreme cases

    c. Your snake of an ex-boyfriend in extreme cases

5. To avoid cracking your paintwork when hanging a picture:

    a. Hammer the nail through masking tape.

    b. Hammer the nail very gently.

    c. Break a nail and get hammered.

Mostly *A*'s: DIY diva!

Congratulations—you have earned your tool belt and are now fully qualified to talk circular saws and cleat nailers with the best of them. Just take it easy before you decide to do a full kitchen remodel.

Mostly *B*'s: Hardware hottie!

You have learned a few tricks but prefer to take the easy road when it comes to getting your hands dirty. We'll let you keep your gadgets, but at least attempt a few jobs on your own before calling in the experts.

Mostly *C*'s: Home wrecker!

You are a DIY disaster. You never have the right tools, and your short bursts of home improvement enthusiasm almost always end badly. Don't blame us when your house falls down around your ears.

Good Times

For those of us who have witnessed a group of guys kicking back, having a smoke, high-fiving each other, giving toasts, and drinking beers, it's clear that men are particularly adept at knowing how to have a good time. Think about it: A woman who loves to have fun, drink cocktails, and live it up is a "party girl." A guy who does the same is simply a guy.

When you want to let your hair down and enjoy a wild night on the town, the number-one thing to remember is this: Hang on to your common sense, but let go of caring about what other people think. Many a night of crazy, unabashed fun has been ruined when a woman either gets hammered in the first two hours of the night (pace yourself!) or refuses to leave her comfort zone within a gaggle of girls. Take a tip from the fellows—nothing ventured, nothing gained. Your real friends will always love you in the morning, hangover and all.

The second thing you need to know is how to enjoy yourself like one of the boys. We recommend learning the tricks of the trade that often make men the life of the party. Whether you're selecting the finest whiskey, smoking a stogie, or slamming back the booze, you will certainly experience a thrilling sense of freedom as you strut into a world where few women dare to venture.

Let the good times roll!

At some point in life, most of us have had to jump out of bed and scramble to make it out of the house at a moment's notice. For most guys, however, this isn't a rare occasion; it's their routine. How do they manage to get ready in five minutes flat? For starters, most guys don't wear makeup, which saves them a lot of time (not to mention money and angst). Second, they concentrate on getting the job done rather than thinking about how they will be perceived. You, too, can master the skill of getting ready in a flash—and still look great—by putting this simple plan in action.

Focus, Focus, Focus

For many women, getting ready in the morning is one of the few times in our day that we get to spend on ourselves. For this reason, we tend to be less-than-focused about the actual task. While we may do things in a certain order, this doesn't necessarily mean we are getting ourselves dressed and presentable in the most efficient order. So when you need to get ready in a snap, you have to toss aside your usual routine and prioritize. What three things can you absolutely not leave the house without doing? Let's say that these are brushing your teeth, combing your hair, and applying deodorant. Is it absolutely necessary for you to take a shower? If not, you just earned yourself bonus time!

Prioritize

Once you've decided which tasks you absolutely can't skip, the next step is to make your plan. If you have lead time, figure out what you are going to wear beforehand and make sure everything you need is in its place. If the situation calls for spontaneous action, simply focus on what you need to accomplish and prioritize your steps.

Time-Sucks and Solutions

Showers. As many men have discovered, when you need to hustle out the door, a shower consumes much more than its fair share of valuable time. Instead, master the PPA (private parts and armpits) technique. Using soap, warm water, and a washcloth, you can come out smelling as sweet as a rose in sixty seconds. Disposable wet wipes will also do in a pinch if you are camping or away from home.

Complex makeup. There's no need to abandon cosmetics altogether in order to meet your five-minute goal. If you frequently find yourself pressed for time in the morning, give yourself a head start

by using salon tints and stains. If you wear mascara, try having your eyelashes professionally dyed. The procedure takes about fifteen minutes and the results last for more than a month. For lively and bright lips, use a red or pink lip stain, available at most cosmetic stores. The color adapts to your lips and will last for hours.

Hair appliances. Using a blow dryer, flat iron, or curling iron is almost out of the question if you're in a rush. Rather than spending time on your usual 'do, pull your hair back in a simple ponytail, parting your hair on the opposite side to counteract any visible bed head. If you have short hair, opt for a crocheted hat or head scarf, both of which are functional and fashionable and can be worn indoors and out.

Ironing. Garments that require pressing are definitely out when you are in a hurry. Choose wash-and-wear outfits, whether you are traveling for business or enjoying recreation time. If your clothes are a wrinkly mess, skip the ironing board. Instead, hang your garment in the shower and use the steam to get out the wrinkles.

More Ways to Beat the Clock! · · · ·

Skip the mirror. Expert "jiffers" tell us that the easiest way for women to get ready in a hustle is to avoid looking in a mirror until the last moment. Mirrors often slow women down by miring them in worries over external judgments or perceptions. Use the mirror only as a disaster check, to make sure you don't have any unsightly stains on your clothes or spinach caught in your teeth.

Pack an emergency bag. Always carry a small "survival" toiletry bag in your purse, stuffed with essentials like tampons, breath mints, wet wipes, and an all-purpose lipstick or gloss. If you are a forgetful person, you may also want to stock your bag with other items, like a spare key or extra cash. This way, you'll never again have to rush back inside to get some essential item that you remembered just as you were sailing out the door.

Apply your makeup on the go. While we always advocate good driving, there is an artful and safe way to put makeup on in the car. First, apply your eye makeup at home. Although it can be done in the car, applying mascara and eyeliner involves timing, a delicate touch, and, of course, your eyes—which should be watching the road! Foundation, blush, and lipstick, on the other hand, are easy to apply at stoplights and while stuck in traffic. Just be sure to have some makeup-removing wipes on hand in case you goof.

Faking It!

Permanent makeup is emerging as an option for those of us who are perpetually pushed for time. Permanent eyeliner, lip liner, full lip color, and brow shading are available. However, if you are always too busy to apply your own lipstick, you probably have bigger time management problems and you may want to consider dropping some activities and working on becoming more organized instead.

I Can... Shine My Shoes!

Nothing ruins the look of a smashing suit or a spectacular outfit like dirty, scuffed shoes. A shoe shine is for a man what a pedicure is for a woman. You'll often see a man kicking back to have his shoes professionally shined on the street or at an airport, but you almost never see a woman pausing to have her heels polished and buffed. We can't give you a definitive reason for this gender difference, but we *can* tell you that well-maintained shoes always make a good impression. If, like many other women, you prefer to shine in the privacy of your own home, here's what you need to do to achieve professional results.

Polish Like a Pro!

If you are serious about maintaining the look and appearance of your shoes, consider investing in a traditional shoe-shine kit. Depending on where you buy it, a decent shoe-shine kit can cost anywhere from $20 to $100. If you decide to go for a deluxe kit, be sure it contains the following essentials:

- Shine and polish brush
- Chamois buffing cloth
- Polish in colors that match your shoes
- Shoehorn

- All-purpose leather cleaner and conditioner

- Storage box with footrest

If you want to get the look of a high-end shoe-shine kit but can't afford the $100 price tag, make your own with these key items:

- Polish brush and old toothbrush

- Standard black and brown polish

- Old, soft T-shirt or cotton socks

- Milk crate (You can store your kit inside it, and turn it upside down for an instant footrest.)

Time to Shine! ··················

Here's how to get that just-shined look.

1. Begin by laying down newspapers on the floor to prevent any polish from staining your floor or work area. Place a thick section of paper off to the side, so you'll have a place to set your shoes to dry when you are finished.

2. Carefully clean away dust and dirt with your brush. Follow with a soft cotton cloth or chamois, wiping off any excess debris. Be sure to get into all the crevices where dust collects.

3. Place your shoes on the footrest or crate. With a circular motion, dab your polish brush in your jar of shoe polish. Spread the polish lightly and evenly across the shoe. Use a cotton swab or toothbrush for small or hard-to-reach areas. Place the shoes on the clean paper and wait fifteen to twenty minutes for the polish to dry.

4. When the shoes are completely dry to the touch, grab your polish brush and begin to wipe off the excess polish. Don't worry—the polish seeps into the porous leather, so you are not undoing your work.

5. Finish by buffing out your shoes with a shine or other cotton cloth or chamois.

When it comes to a great shoe shine, you can't take any short cuts. Every step of the procedure is essential. So relax, indulge your desire for beautiful shoes, and give yourself the shine you deserve!

Faking It!

For a quick fix, use vegetable oil on a soft cloth to buff out unsightly scuff marks. To hide scrapes on shoes that are an unusual color, fill in the scratches with an ink marker in a matching hue.

I Can... Tie a Tie!

You may not be going for Diane Keaton's Oscar-night look, but there are many reasons for women to know how to tie a tie. First of all, it's fun. Completing a good knot is satisfying. It's also a skill with grace—you can always help your father, husband, son, or friend as a gesture of kindness. Finally, it's just cool. The ability to tie a tie in a fashionable manner is perennially *en vogue.*

The first thing you need to know about tying a tie is that not all knots are created equal. In fact, there are four standard knots you need to know: the four-in-hand, the Windsor, the half Windsor, and the Pratt (also sometimes referred to as the Shelby). The knot you choose depends entirely on what kind of look the wearer is trying to project.

To keep it simple, we will refer to the widest part of the tie as the fat, or F, leg and the narrowest part of the tie as the skinny, or S, leg.

Four-in-Hand Knot · · · · · · · · · · · · ·

The four-in-hand is the basic tie knot, appropriate for semiformal occasions.

1. Drape the tie around your neck. F should extend about 12 inches below S. Cross F over S.

2. Turn F back underneath S.

3. Bring F back over in front of S again.

4. Pull F up and through the loop around your neck.

5. Pinch the front of the knot loosely with your index finger and thumb and thread F down through the front loop.

6. Carefully remove your finger and gently tighten the knot to the collar by holding S and sliding the knot up.

Windsor Knot · · · · · · · · · · · · · · · · · · ·

For formal occasions, the Windsor is the knot to go with. This knot is also a great choice for people with longer necks, because the wide style balances the longer proportion of the neck.

1. Drape the tie around your neck. F should extend about 12 inches below S. Cross F over S.

2. Pull F up through the loop between the collar and tie, and then back down.

3. Bring F underneath S and to the left, and back through the loop you have now created.

4. Bring F across the front from left to right.

5. Bring F up through the loop again.

6. Pull F down through the knot in front.

7. Using both hands, tighten the knot carefully and draw up to the collar.

Half Windsor Knot · · · · · · · · · · · · · ·

This more-casual brother of the Windsor knot looks best on wide ties.

1. Drape the tie around your neck. F should extend about 12 inches below S. Cross F over S.

2. Pull F up around and behind S.

3. Bring F up and through the loop.

4. Take F around front, over S from left to right.

5. Again, bring F up and thread it down through the knot in front.

6. Using both hands, tighten the knot carefully and draw up to the collar.

Pratt (or Shelby) Knot ···········

Slightly wider and looser than the Windsor, the Pratt is the modern person's tie knot (illustrated at right).

1. Start with the tie draped around your neck inside out, with *F* under *S* and *F* slightly longer than *S*.

2. Take *F* over and under *S*.

3. Pull the loop (the twisted bit) down and tighten.

4. Take *F* over to the left again.

5. Bring *F* up, behind the loop.

6. Pull *F* through the knot in front and gently tighten. The tip of *F* should just touch the top of your belt buckle.

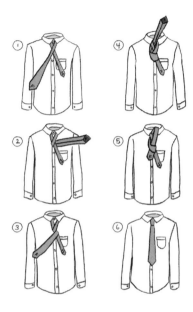

Random Fact: The necktie first became popular when Louis XIV admired the fabric band that Croatian soldiers wore around their necks. Many believe the word *cravat* is derived from the French *Croatta*.

I Can... Avoid Chores (and Not Feel Guilty)!

Men are particularly adept at dodging mundane tasks that might hamper an evening of play. Unfortunately, women aren't blessed with the same mental escape button. We tend to allow ourselves to have fun only *after* the laundry is done. So the next time you're ramping up to a big night of fun, follow these simple suggestions and leave the chores to someone else.

Excuses, Excuses

The truth is, as women we have been taught that we are responsible for the care and keeping of our spaces. No matter where or with whom we live, if a space is untidy, we tend to see it as our failure. Men do not experience this feeling of failure, because they don't feel responsible in the first place. The best way to avoid feeling responsible for chores is to procrastinate and think of myriad better ways to spend your time. Chores are a serious buzz kill, so why not put them off to a time when you don't need all of your energy reserves?

The dishes can wait, the bills can wait, the clutter in your bathroom cabinet can wait. A messy house is not a reflection of you. It's just an indication that you are having too much fun to care.

Value Your Time

Another way men slip out of doing everyday tasks is by actually attaching a value to their time. This is a lesson we should learn. Whether you are working inside or outside the home, your time is valuable. Think about how much you make per hour and weigh it against the chore at hand. Is it really worth $30 an hour for you to clean toilets? We didn't think so. If you can afford it, hire a professional service and save yourself a great deal of time, money, and important mental energy.

Now that your toilets are being cleaned by someone else and you have received permission to forgo all unpleasant chores, get out there and have fun!

GIRL'S WORLD

Next time your sloppy roommate lets the dishes pile up in the sink, call on an old frat house trick. Place the undone dishes on her bed pillow. This is a sure-fire remedy for reminding her just how gross it is to let the dishes go.

I Can... Slam a Drink!

While we don't advocate binge drinking, we certainly must honor the art of downing a beer in less than thirty seconds. All this remarkable feat requires is a can of beer, a sharp utensil, and, of course, a wild and reckless streak. The rest is left to gravity. Oh, and we do recommend that you wear a towel as a bib on your first attempt, because you will almost certainly get soaked.

Gone in Thirty Seconds

1. On a sturdy table, place your beer can on its side. Using a clean, sharp object like a screwdriver, awl, sturdy pen, or key, puncture a hole in the side of the can about an inch from the base in line with the mouthpiece. Place your thumb over the hole to ensure no beer is spilled (on your pretty pink bouse).

2. Bring the can up to your mouth and place your mouth tightly over the hole. Quickly open the top of the can with your other hand.

3. Tip your head back at a nearly 90-degree angle from your body. Tilt the can, aiming it so it will pour directly down your throat. It is easier to keep the can vertical.

4. Let gravity take its course!

Don't be surprised if the crowd surrounding you chants, "Chug, chug, chug," as the beer falls straight down the chute and the can is empty before you can come up for air.

Old School ·

If downing a can of beer in less than a minute sounds like a college prank, you may prefer the manly whiskey slam. Begin by bellying up to the bar (for best results, exercise this move at a salty, 1940s-style steak-house bar). Ask the bartender for a Jameson straight up. When he brings it out, hand him a folded fiver, exhale deeply, and literally throw the entire drink into the back of your mouth without stopping. When you're finished, slam the glass back on the table, wipe your lips, and say, "Ah!"

The Thrill of the Chase · · · · · · · · · · ·

For those occasions when a shot hits the spot, don't be afraid to order up a chaser to balance the flavor of whatever hard alcohol you decide to pound. Whether you opt for something rich and sweet like Kahlúa or tart and acidic like an orange wedge, a good chaser can make just about anything go down smooth.

EXTRA CREDIT!

A perfect finish to slamming a can of beer is to smash the can on your forehead. Place the butt of the beer can on your forehead and pinch the sides in order to allow the can to collapse; this way it won't leave a mark on your head. Using the heel of your palm, smash the can and make an appropriately loud grunting noise or roar.

I Can... Whistle for a Cab!

You might think that hailing a cab is self-explanatory, but there is indeed an art to it. Many cabbies simply won't pick up people who seem hesitant, rude, or don't follow protocol. Basic cab-hailing procedure includes standing at the curb, watching for the illuminated numbers that indicate the cab is available, and making a clear hand motion to get the driver's attention. Sometimes these steps don't do the trick, so you have to whistle. You know how to whistle, don't you?

Two-Finger Whistle

A whistle is a sound that is produced when a stream of air is divided and therefore vibrates. While there are many different whistling techniques, the one-handed "taxi" whistle is by far the coolest. Bring the tips of your thumb and middle fingers together, loosely forming the letter o. Insert your fingers into your mouth, just past your teeth and under the tip of your tongue. Relax the rest of your arm and let it hang down. Blow, while experimenting with various degrees of tension between your fingers. Hear that? It's the start of a full-blown whistle!

EXTRA WHISTLE!

If you haven't already mastered the two-fingered whistle, why not put a whistle on your keychain—a multi-purpose tool for both hailing a cab and staying safe on the street.

I Can... Make a Toast!

The ability to make a wise and heartfelt toast is a fine asset. A good toast can kick off a celebration, move a crowd, and bring happiness to the individual who is the subject of the toast.

Prepare Your Sentiments

Brainstorm a list of every thought and emotion that comes to mind when you envision the person or couple you are speaking about—words, phrases, and inside jokes. Consider what makes the occasion you are toasting special or unique. Also, be yourself. Many people make the mistake of hunting for quotes from famous people in history. Why use the words of a stranger when the most meaningful and powerful sentiments come from your own experience?

You'll want to keep your audience in mind when you're writing your speech. If you don't know who is going to be in attendance, ask for a guest list. As you review the people's names, think about what kind of toast they would want to hear. Would the bride's grandma feel comfortable hearing about her grand-daughter's drunken shenanigans, for example?

To make your toast really memorable, include the following elements:

- Add sincere and personal compliments about the special qualities and traits of the subject of your toast.

- Start the speech with a question or meaningful anecdote that you answer or finish at the end.

- Do not forget the object of the toast. Conclude by asking everyone to raise a glass and dedicate your words to the person and/or occasion at hand.

Stage a Dress Rehearsal ········

Once you've written your toast, practice your speech and commit it to memory until you know it backward and forward. That way, if you lose your notes, you can still feel confident because it's all right there upstairs, in your mind.

A day or two before the event, work out any bugs and defeat the element of your own surprise by rehearsing your toast in the setting—and even the clothes, if possible—in which you plan to make it. This will give you a sense of the space and acoustics and allow you to get comfortable with the whole idea. If the event will take place in a hotel ballroom or restaurant, ask the employees if you can have a few minutes to yourself in the room to practice your speech.

While you're rehearsing, tap into the power that comes with visualizing your own success. Imagine how your friend will feel when you recount all of the special things she has done for you. Picture the audience smiling and nodding as they listen to your well-constructed and creative speech.

Giving the Toast ················

You're likely to be a little jittery when the time finally comes for you to perform. Getting nervous about being nervous is a common experience. Everyone feels uneasy sometimes; it's normal, natural, and quite endearing. Instead of feeling overwhelmed by it, use that nervous energy to your advantage. The extra dose of adrenaline can help you stay focused on and excited about what you are saying, and this is a great thing. Remember that it's an honor to be asked to make this very important toast. The toastee wouldn't have asked you if she didn't think you could do it, so relax and take a deep breath. It's not like you're delivering the State of the Union address.

Finally, don't apologize, no matter what happens. Nothing kills a speech or toast like an apology. Making excuses undermines your authority as a speaker and makes your entire audience feel uncomfortable. Speak the flattering truth. Own what you say and be proud to say it.

I Can... Punch Someone!

Isn't it satisfying when the bad guy gets socked in the face in your favorite action film? It's especially fun to see a woman deck a villain, but is it something that only happens in the movies?

The truth is, you don't need to be built like a brick house to serve up a forceful strike. Throwing a good punch mostly requires balance, practice, technique, and a major dose of adrenaline.

Find Your Stance

The first thing you need to do is to assume a strong stance. This is achieved by finding your center of gravity. Stand with your feet shoulder-width apart. Place the majority of your weight on the balls of your feet. With your feet firmly on the ground, pivot the upper half of your body from side to side. Imagine that someone wants to push you over, and you need to ground yourself in a way that would make it nearly impossible. Once you've found this position, you've got your stance.

Strike a Pose

Turn your body so that your strongest side (generally the right side, if you are right handed) is closest to your opponent. Remember, you want your opponent to have the smallest possible strike zone, so make the side of your body long and lean by standing side on to your opponent instead of face on.

Now it's time to make a fist. A common mistake when making a fist is to tuck your thumb inside your fist. Instead, wrap your thumb around the outside of your knuckles. Once your fist is secure and ready, bring it up to your face but in line with your arm. Take the "guard" position, blocking the side of your face with the top of your knuckles just underneath your eye.

Draw on Your Core Strength · · · · ·

When throwing a punch, it's important to move from your abdomen in order to harness your core strength. The power of your punch does not come from the strength of your shoulder or bicep, but from the force of your body executing a complete motion.

Throw the Punch · · · · · · · · · · · · · · ·

Now it's time to stand and deliver. To do this, you need to decide on your point of contact, or where you want to strike your opponent. If you are just sparring or having a good time, you may choose the shoulder. However, if you wish to stupefy and stun your opponent, you'll need to deal a blow to the face or stomach.

Ready? Pivot your strong side back and draw your arm and shoulder back. Now follow through with your arm and fist to the point of contact. You should imagine yourself actually trying to hit through the point of contact on your opponent's body and out the other side in one imaginary and forceful line. For extra power, yell or exhale deeply as you strike. Bring your arm back immediately into guard position if you are sparring. If you're not sparring and this was a self-protective punch, do what you need to do make yourself as small a target as possible, including getting away from your opponent altogether.

You can practice your punches on a punching bag or old couch cushion. Or you can buy an inexpensive bag of animal feed or birdseed at your local pet supply store and wail on it until it breaks.

I Can... Open a Beer without a Bottle Opener!

Those of us who choose not to carry a bottle opener on our key chain may sometimes find ourselves in the company of an unopened bottle. On these occasions, it's important to remember that a bottle can be opened with many easily found items and does not require a wussy dime-store apparatus. Try any of the tricks below to impress your friends and quench your thirst.

Your Fist

Find a hard, flat surface that can handle a nick or scuff or two. Hold the bottle perpendicular to the surface, with the lip of the bottle cap resting on the edge of the surface.

Slam your fist firmly and directly down on the bottle cap. You may need to try this a few times in order to get it to work. The metal bottle cap should fan out so you can easily remove it if it doesn't pop off altogether.

Keys

Using a set of keys to open a bottle is not for the inexperienced or the impatient. A set of keys can be used in either of two ways. One option is to slip a large key ring over the bottle cap and harness one side of the cap, pulling toward the opposite side until the cap loosens and comes off. The other option is to use a single key to slowly pry off the top. By hooking the teeth of the key under the lip of the cap all the way around, you will bend and loosen the cap until it eventually comes off. (Use a nonessential or easily replaceable key, since it may get damaged in the process.)

A Fire Hydrant · · · · · · · · · · · · · · · · ·

While not the most practical means of
removing a bottle cap, the fire hydrant
trick is definitely an attention getter.
Place the cap in the small recess between
the screw and the nut on the "teat" of the
hydrant and pop off the top. Be sure to
look around and notice who might have
witnessed you pulling off this totally
super-cool move.

Your Belt Buckle (or Someone Else's) ·

The belt buckle is by far the sexiest of
all the ersatz bottle openers. In fact, we
urge you to try this move at a party where
an opener is in plain sight. If you are not
wearing a belt yourself, well, then you'll
just have to find the nearest cowboy or
hipster (whichever suits your fancy) to
supply the buckle. Place the bottle cap
inside the buckle frame. Using the
buckle as a lever, pop the top. Savor
that magical moment when your bottle
is open and some cute guy's pants
are unbuckled.

Nothing represents celebration, success, and achievement quite as boldly as smoking a fine cigar with friends. Becoming a cigar aficionado is easy—you just need to know how to choose, light, and puff your stogie.

Make Your Choice

While there are hundreds of different cigar types, cigars fall into three major categories, which are based on size and shape:

Panatela: Long and slim

Corona: The classic shape with one rounded end

Figuardo: More exotic, with irregular shapes

If you have never smoked a cigar before, we recommend choosing something long and thin, since the size and shape of a cigar has a direct relationship to its intensity. Thinner cigars tend to stay cooler and have less intense smoke.

Choosing a cigar of high quality will make your experience much more pleasant. Of course, authentic Cuban cigars are known for their excellence, but it is illegal for American citizens to buy or obtain them, even when visiting other countries. So, since smoking a good Havana is not an option, consult the following tips to identify a high-quality cigar.

- Squeeze your cigar to make sure there are no lumps—which would be a sign that the tobacco is of low quality.

- Don't buy a cigar if the paper around it or the tobacco at the end looks discolored. The cigar paper should be taut and have the color of cardboard. The tobacco should be dark and fresh looking.

- Only buy cigars that are 100 percent tobacco, with no additives. If you are unsure, ask a shopkeeper for help.

Cut the Cigar · · · · · · · · · · · · · · · · · · ·

If you purchase your cigar from a fine tobacco shop, you may ask them to cut the head (the end closest to the band) off for you. You should only cut it, however, if you plan to smoke the cigar in the next several hours. Otherwise, the tobacco will dry out slightly and alter the taste. If you won't be smoking your cigar until later, you'll need to buy a single- or double-blade cutter so you can cut the head off the cigar yourself when you're

ready to smoke it. A sharp paring knife will do in a pinch.

To cut the cigar, simply place your cutter directly over the end and cut firmly, pushing the blade straight down like a guillotine.

Light the Cigar · · · · · · · · · · · · · · · · · · ·

Choosing the proper lighting instrument is just as important as selecting the right cigar, since it affects the flavor of your smoke. Do not use matches to light a cigar; they contain ammonia, which will taint the aroma and taste of the cigar. Instead, purchase a lighter made specifically for lighting cigars.

Put the head of the cigar in your mouth and light the end as you gently pull the smoke into your mouth (but not into your lungs). You'll need to puff several times until the end of the cigar is sufficiently lit.

Enjoy the Cigar · · · · · · · · · · · · · · · · · ·

Unlike you would when smoking a
cigarette or other dried leaf product,
don't inhale the smoke from your cigar.
Instead, draw the smoke into the cham-
ber of your mouth, enjoying the subtle
taste and aroma of the smoke before
puffing it out. It's customary to take ten
to twelve puffs before removing the foil
cigar band (it often falls off from the heat
about this time anyway). For full enjoy-
ment, pair your cigar with a nice glass
of well-aged cabernet sauvignon, port,
cognac, or scotch.

GIRL'S WORLD

The next time you are having a
bunch of friends over for a girls'
night in, consider bringing out a
box of fine cigars to smoke after
dinner. For decades, men have
talked about business, politics,
and philosophy over a nice cigar.
Why not do the same? Serve with
cognac or brandy and, who knows,
you might just solve all the world's
problems!

Drinking whiskey may sound hard core, but to those in the know, selecting and sipping this complex liquor is a refined art. Whiskey comes in several different forms, each of which has its own unique history, taste, and fan base. Whole books are written on the origins of different whiskeys, but we'll save you the trouble by providing the basic facts, below.

Types of Whiskey

Whiskey differs by type depending on what grain or "mash" (combination of grains) it is made from. Selecting a whiskey depends on your personal taste. The descriptions below may help you zero in on your whiskey of choice.

Single Malt. Ironically, single-malt whiskey is made from a combination of malted grains that form a mash. The word *single* in the name actually indicates that the whiskey was made and bottled at a single distillery. Single malts are generally the best and most expensive whiskeys, because they bear the unique characteristics associated with the distillery that made them.

Straight. Like the name suggests, straight whiskey is quite strong. The best straight whiskey is aged in charred oak barrels until it reaches its full potential—in some cases for twenty-five years. Straight whiskey is never less than 80 proof (40 percent alcohol by volume).

Blended. Blended whiskey is made from straight whiskey mixed with neutral spirits. Of the three types of whiskey, blended tends to have the most mellow flavor and can often be enjoyed without diluting it with water or ice.

How to Enjoy ·

To get the full whiskey experience, take some tips from the experts:

• While whiskey is often combined with other spirits to make cocktails such as manhattans or Rob Roys, most true whiskey lovers say it's best with just a splash of water.

• Whiskey is best enjoyed from a tulip-shaped glass that allows you to experience the flavor and aroma of the drink.

• If you don't know which brand names are best, you can make sure that you're ordering a high-quality whiskey by asking how many years it's been aged—the longer the better.

Type	Country or State	Grain	Minimum Age (years)	Best Age (years)
Scotch	Scotland	Barley	3	8–25
Irish	Ireland	Barley	3	8–25
Bourbon	Kentucky	Corn	2	5–8
Tennessee	Tennessee	Corn	2	4–5
Canadian	Canada	Rye	4	5–8

You can cure your own cold, or at least have fun trying. Next time you are feeling under the weather, try this age-old remedy—the Hot Toddy. Pour 1½ ounces of whiskey, 3 ounces of hot water, and a teaspoon each of lemon juice and honey into a glass mug. Blend the ingredients together and drink it down to ease your sore throat and help you sleep through the night.

Are You a Woman about Town or Just a Clown?

1. A PPA "shower" is

   a. The fastest way to get yourself clean when you are in a rush

   b. A monthly meeting to welcome the newest members of Party Planners of America

   c. A new hydrotherapy treatment offered by only the hippest spas

2. Which one of the following is a type of tie knot?

   a. Windsor

   b. Carrington

   c. Trollop

3. To conquer nerves before making a toast:

   a. Stage a dress rehearsal.

   b. Drink a large scotch.

   c. Stage your own death.

4. The sexiest way to open a bottle is with

   a. A belt buckle

   b. Your teeth

   c. Someone else's teeth

5. Where does bourbon originally come from?

   a. Kentucky

   b. Scotland

   c. New Hampshire

Scoring

Mostly *A*'s: Woman about town!

You know how to have a good time and you look great doing it. You should be on everybody's party list!

Mostly *B*'s: Rising star!

You're a social animal who just needs a little bit of training. We recommend brushing up on your barroom skills before the next happy hour.

Mostly *C*'s: In the gutter!

You are a walking faux pas. We suggest staying home and reviewing this chapter more closely before you hit the gentlemen's club—or any club.

Gearhead

Once upon a time, not so long ago, the public education system was set up in such a way that the sexes were overtly separated and differentiated. High school girls studied home economics, so that they could learn to make a pound cake and whip up a snazzy pair of curtains. Boys, on the other hand, were automatically registered for shop class, where they would get down and dirty, fix cars, and use power saws. Today, schools are less sexist in their curricula, but the gap in learning remains.

There will be times in life when you find yourself stuck in a ditch wishing you knew how to change a tire or fix a bicycle chain. For just these occasions, we have compiled a number of "gear head" skills that are easy to learn and can truly save your life. From jump-starting a car to driving a stick shift, you can master the key automotive secrets that men have been hoarding for years. The truth is, they're just not that hard, and you don't even need to wear coveralls. But do smear some grease on your face, just for effect.

If you want to be a chick who can tell the difference between a V-6 and a V-4 and ride your own Harley, then roll up your sleeves, open your mind, and start your engine!

I Can . . . Jump-start a Car!

Dead batteries usually happen at the worst times. In fact, is there ever a good time for a car to refuse to start? Prepare yourself for this situation by investing in a good pair of heavy-gauge jumper cables and store them in your trunk. Get cables that are at least 10 feet long so that they can reach a second car when you need them most. It's also a good idea to buy some safety goggles to keep in the trunk with your cables; jump-starting a car is pretty easy, but you'll want to keep your eyes protected from any flying sparks or hazardous materials.

The next time you come back to your car to find that the battery has kicked the bucket, the first thing you'll need to do is find a friend or trustworthy person. If you are relying on the kindness of strangers, we recommend enlisting the help of a woman, for safety reasons.

Locate the Battery

Begin by opening the hood of your car and looking for the battery, which is usually located in the middle of the engine and resembles a rectangular box. You will recognize the battery by its markings indicating its make and voltage.

Check the Battery ··············

All batteries contain a potent electrolyte solution containing sulfuric acid. *If there is any chance that this solution could be frozen, do not jump-start the car—the battery could explode. Call for professional help.*

Be sure to check the condition of the plastic casing on both your own battery and the battery that will give you the jump start. If the casing is cracked or damaged or you cannot determine the voltage, do not proceed any further. Call for help and be sure to replace the damaged battery as soon as possible. It's normal for batteries to have a small amount of blue or green "snow" surrounding the battery terminals. If this is the case, use a cloth or small wire brush to clean the battery. Do not wipe it off with your bare hands, because the chemical solution is corrosive and could harm your skin.

Check to make sure the voltage on both batteries matches. Unless you are getting a jump start off a '57 Chevy, the voltage on both cars will probably be the same.

Next, we'll move on to attaching the jumper cables to the batteries. But before you start, make sure your helper's car is turned off and that the cars are not touching each other.

Attach the Jumper Cables ·······

Each battery has two terminals, which are marked with symbols to indicate whether the charge is positive (+) or negative (-). It is vital that you follow the instructions below in the exact order when attaching cables (see the diagram on page 154).

1. Attach one end of the red jumper cable to the dead battery's positive terminal. Next, attach the other end of that jumper cable to the starting vehicle's positive terminal.

2. Attach one end of the black cable to the negative terminal of the starting vehicle's battery. Attach the other end to a metal bolt on the engine block of the car with the dead battery. Make sure that the cable is attached to the block and not to the battery itself.

starting
Car

dead
Car

engine block or frame

TURBO

Start the Car ·

Once the cables are in place, start the car that is providing the jump and let it run for five minutes. Now you can try starting the car with the dead battery. If it doesn't start within thirty seconds, wait another five minutes before trying again. If it still won't start, you will need to call for a tow truck.

Remove the Cables · · · · · · · · · · · · · ·

Once the car with the dead battery has been up and running for a few minutes, you can remove the starter cables in the opposite order in which you attached them. In other words, remove first the negative from the dead battery block, then the negative from the starting car, then the positive from the starting car, and finally the positive from the previously dead battery.

Pay Your Dues ··················

It's a good idea to offer your friend or Good Samaritan a small honorarium for helping you out. A reasonable gesture would be $10 to $20 (although chances are that the person won't accept it). Consider this a small token compared to the amount of money you would have had to pay a garage or towing service to help you out. And remember, for good car karma, you're now obliged to help another stalled driver.

Now you're prepared for a battery-related emergency! So when you need to jump-start your car, you won't have to rely on someone else's knowledge or cables— you'll have it all close at hand.

GIRL'S WORLD

Why not learn what the guys did back in junior high? Look for a car-maintenance class at your local community college. Think of the looks you will get when you can tell a guy how to properly lube his chassis!

I Can... *Drive a Stick Shift!*

Okay, so no driving school has ever suggested learning how to drive by reading a cute book like this one. Still, the basics of driving a stick can be easily digested through these well-crafted instructions. Many women never learn how to drive a manual transmission because they are intimidated by all those gears, not to mention the horrifying prospect of stalling at an intersection. We're here to tell you that with a little know-how and a whole lot of practice, you'll be able to push in the clutch and put the pedal to the metal in no time!

Know Thy Gears

We recommend finding a friend or relative with a not-so-expensive, older car and an abundance of patience and positive energy. You can begin your first lesson by simply sitting in the driver's seat of the car and familiarizing yourself with the landscape.

There are three pedals on the floorboard of a car with a manual transmission. You will be using two feet, not one, when you drive a stick shift. From left to right you will find the clutch, the brake, and the gas pedal. The clutch is the pedal that allows you to change gears manually (a job that is done for you in a car with an automatic transmission).

Next, study the simple illustration on the top of the gearshift that shows you the position of the gears. Although this illustration may differ depending on the make and model of your car, it will mostly likely look like a three-legged H. The odd-numbered gears (first, third, and fifth) are at the top. The even-numbered gears (second, fourth) are at the bottom, along with Reverse. The neutral gear is the cross bar of the H. Note that not all cars have a fifth gear.

Zen and the Art of Gear Shifting

When you are feeling confident and are ready to set the car in motion, start in an area such as a parking lot that is flat and has plenty of open space. Be sure that the parking brake is engaged and that your seat belts, and those of your passengers, are securely fastened.

1. With the car turned off, press down on the clutch with your left foot and move the gear shift into the neutral position. Start the car. With your left foot still pushing the clutch pedal down, shift into first gear by moving the gear shift all the way to the left and up.

2. With your right foot, apply the foot brake, then release the parking brake.

3. Slowly begin to release the clutch, paying close attention to the feeling and sound of the engine. When you sense—by hearing and/or feeling— the engine beginning to slow down, gently press the gas pedal and release the clutch completely. Think of it as a see-saw motion between the gas and clutch pedals. The car will then move forward. Don't worry if it's a little jerky at first; you will eventually learn how to make a smooth transition. If you stall, simply put the car in neutral and start over again.

4. When the car is in motion, you can accelerate in first gear until the engine reaches about 3,000 rpm; you'll be able to monitor this by watching the dials on the dashboard. With practice, you will no longer need to look at the dashboard display—you will simply sense when it's time to shift.

5. To shift into second, gently take your foot off the gas, press down on the clutch pedal and pull the gearshift all the way down into second gear. Release the clutch pedal gently while applying pressure to the gas pedal.

6. Repeat the shifting process each time you hit the next 3,000 rpm marker, until you're driving at the appropriate speed.

7. When you want to gradually decrease your speed, slowly lift your foot off the gas. Then downshift by simply pressing down on the clutch, moving the gearshift to a lower gear, and slowly releasing the clutch as you reengage the gas. Repeat down through the gears to slow as needed. When you're ready to stop, once you're in first gear, release the clutch slowly and gently brake.

8. To stop the car quickly, simply depress the clutch and step on the brake. When you're ready to park, keeping your foot on the clutch, put the gearshift into neutral or first gear (the latter is recommended, just in case your parking brake fails) and turn off the car.

Top Tips for Beginners ···········

• To drive in reverse, follow the exact same steps you would take to start in first gear. Note that the reverse gear engages more quickly than first gear does, so make sure you release the clutch slowly, and gently apply the gas as soon as the car moves.

• When starting on an incline, follow the advice of many driving experts, who suggest keeping the parking brake on while you press on the gas, then releasing it after you begin transitioning to the clutch. This allows you to engage the clutch without the fear of rolling into the car behind or in front of you.

- Be safe, not self-conscious. Give yourself plenty of time and space to practice your driving skills. Once you have mastered the basics, slowly make your way into areas with other motorists. If you stall, it's not a big deal. Take a deep breath and try, try again.

- If you are concerned about damaging the transmission of your friend's car while you're learning, take a lesson from a professional driving school. A few hours of driver training and you'll be ready to hit the road.

- Treat yourself to a free stick-shift driving lesson by observing a friend who drives a car with a manual transmission. Pay close attention as she starts the car, feel the sound of the engine revving, and watch carefully as she shifts gears.

Faking It!

If you find yourself confronted with a manual transmission car and have no idea how to drive it, get in second gear and stay there. It's not so great for the car and you won't be able to drive very fast, but you will save face, and that's the important thing.

I Can... *Parallel Park!*

In the classic movie *Annie Hall*, a harried Diane Keaton screeches her VW bug through the streets of Manhattan before crookedly pulling headfirst into a parking space. Her passenger, Woody Allen, gets out and says, "No problem. I can walk to the curb from here." Don't be another sad cliché of womankind. Learn how to park like a pro by following this foolproof parking tutorial.

Park It

1. Stake a claim on your parking spot. If a car is about to leave but the spot isn't vacant yet, simply wait behind the spot (with your turn signal on), allowing enough room for the vacating car to get out. As soon as the space is empty, pull ahead of it far enough so that your rear bumper is lined up with the rear bumper of the car parked in front of your space, keeping a distance of about 2 feet between you and the parked car.

2. Put the car in reverse and begin backing up slowly. When the car begins to move, turn the steering wheel toward the curb as far as it will go. Slowly angle back into the space. When your car's front door is even with the rear bumper of the parked car beside you, stop reversing and turn the wheel away from the curb. With the wheel turned away from the curb, continue backing into the space until your car is nearly in line with the cars ahead of and behind you.

3. Finally, straighten the wheel out and pull forward. Your car should be 6 to 8 inches from the curb when you are parked.

Curb Your Enthusiasm · · · · · · · · · · ·

If you are parking on an incline and your car is pointing uphill, before you turn off the car, turn your steering wheel all the way to the left so the wheels are turned away from the curb. If your car is pointing downhill, turn your wheel all the way to the right so the wheels are turned into the curb. This will prevent your car from rolling if the parking brake should fail.

EXTRA CREDIT!

Learn how to get in and out of tight spots by setting up cones or making chalk marks on the street and practicing your parallel parking. Before you know it, you will be maneuvering your station wagon as if it were a Fiat!

I Can... Change a Tire!

Changing a tire on your own may sound like a colossal hassle, but it is a very important skill for any adventurous female traveler to have in her back pocket. After all, if you are road-tripping in the south of France, who will you call to save your *derrière* when your tire catches a flat? Become your own best roadside assistance program!

If at all possible, be sure that you begin the tire-changing process on solid, flat ground. If you are on any kind of incline, jam a heavy object like a rock or brick into the downhill side of the other tire on that side of the car (the rear, if you're changing a front tire, and the front, if changing a rear tire). Make sure your parking brake is on so that the car does not accidentally roll. Have your passengers stay inside the car if you are on a busy highway.

How to Change a Tire

1. First, remove the spare tire, lugwrench, and jack from the trunk of the car. This necessary equipment is generally stowed underneath the floor of the trunk. Place the jack under the metal portion of the frame near the tire that you are going to change. (If you put the jack under any other portion of the frame, you will run the risk of cracking the body when you start lifting.) Consult your owner's manual for instructions on the exact placement of the jack.

2. Before you attempt to jack up the car, remove the hubcap with the crowbar end of the lugwrench and loosen the lug nuts with the wrench end so they're about halfway unscrewed. Now, pump the jack to lift the car until the tire is off the ground. Finish loosening the nuts and remove them and then the tire. Place the nuts in the hubcap to prevent them from rolling away.

3. Put the spare tire on the wheel and screw on the nuts, using the lugwrench or your finger, giving each one only a full turn or two until they are equally tight. Then tighten each nut individually with the wrench—as firmly as possible. You are allowed to jump on the wrench to do this.

4. Lower the car to the ground fully, and remove the jack. Tighten the nuts again. Replace the hubcap, and you're finished!

Be sure to take the flat tire with you; some punctures can be repaired. And remember, you can only drive on your small spare, or "dinky," for about one hundred miles, and you can't go over the speed of 50 mph while driving on it.

Now get yourself to a tire shop to replace or repair that punctured tire, and don't hesitate to let 'em know that you changed the tire yourself!

The Jargon

Dinky or **donut:** The small spare tire that is generally found under the floor mat of your car trunk

Lug wrench: A special wrench used to remove and replace the lug nuts on a hubcap. It's wise to carry one in the trunk of your car for easy tire changes.

You've just bought a piece of unassembled furniture, or perhaps a fully assembled coffee table you can't live without. Now, how do you fit it in your Mini Cooper? If you don't have a roof rack and you need to haul something a short distance, you can tie it to the top of your car. Tying gear down is easy: All you need is two strong knots and a whole lot of elbow grease. Follow these instructions next time you need to mount something securely and safely to the roof of your car.

Before you start, get yourself a blanket or large carpet with rubber backing on one side, at least two pieces of nylon rope (about 20 feet each in length), and someone (maybe yourself!) who can tie bowline and half hitch knots (see "I Can . . . Tie Knots!" page 200). We recommend carrying these supplies in the trunk of your car at all times in case of a furniture bargain emergency!

Tie One On

1. Fold your blanket so that it is flat and has roughly the same dimensions as the roof of your car.

2. Center the blanket on the roof, with the rubber backing (if any) facing down, and place your object on top. Remember that weight shifts easily when the car is moving, so be sure to balance your load. For example, if you are carrying a chair, place it on its back so that the heaviest part of the chair is against the roof.

3. Run both lengths of nylon rope across and, if possible, through your object. One rope should be near the front doors of the car, and the other near the rear doors. Open the car doors and pull the rope ends down through each door frame.

4. Tie a bowline at one end of each rope.

5. Next, put the remaining ends of the ropes inside the car, and pull the unknotted end of one rope through the loop of the bowline in that rope. Then shift the entire length of rope so that the bowline is on top of the car.

6. Yank down on the unknotted end of the rope. The loop of the bowline will act like a pulley and allow you to create the tension to cinch the knot. Tug until the rope is as taut as possible.

7. To tie it off, make two half hitches below the bowline.

8. Repeat with the other rope to secure both sides to the roof.

9. Finally, close all four doors, making sure that any leftover or dangling rope is tucked inside the car. Otherwise the knots may become loose and/or the ropes get tangled in the tires.

Faking It!

You can quickly and easily secure equipment such as bikes or luggage to the top of your car using bungee cords, available at hardware stores. Simply strap your object to the car and stretch the cords inside until the ends meet, and hook them together. You can also hook the bungee cord ends to the inside of your door or trunk. Use bungee cords with plastic-coated hooks so you won't damage or scratch your car.

I Can... Drive a Truck!

The truck is an icon of American culture, the modern equivalent of the horse of the old West. With their tough image, trucks are often portrayed in movies and TV commercials as vehicles made for adventure.

But there are many times in life when you need a truck for utilitarian purposes. Whether you are moving furniture or just need to haul some serious bargains home from the flea market, a truck is a handy mode of transportation. Many women rely on male friends or hire professionals, but the dirty secret about driving a truck isn't so dirty: If you can drive a car, you can drive a truck.

A Truck for Every Season

Trucks come in all shapes and sizes, so let's review the basics. These are the types of trucks you can drive with a standard driver's license:

Pickup truck. Pickups are the most accessible and easiest to drive in the lineup of trucks. Choose full-size or compact, depending on your hauling needs.

Cargo van. A cargo van does not have a separate cab but offers one continuous loading space.

Stake-bed or flatbed truck. A stake-bed truck takes its name from its open platform bed, to which you stake or tie your cargo.

Box truck. Most trucks you see driving through neighborhoods making deliveries are box trucks. Box trucks come in many different sizes, most of which can be rented from a local agency.

No matter which type of truck you drive, remember the importance of a balanced load. If you are moving furniture, be sure to secure it to the wall or bed of the truck. Use boxes and blankets to fill in any gaps so that your load does not move, shake, or come loose as you travel down the road.

How to Keep On Truckin' · · · · · · · · ·

The central differences between driving a car and a truck are the mirrors, the transmission, and the clearance. Here's what you need to keep in mind:

Mirrors. Backing up a truck is different from backing up a car-because you do not always have a back window to look out of. Instead, you must rely on the rectangular mirrors that are positioned on each side of the front door of your truck. If you are using an older truck, you may need to adjust the mirrors manually; newer truck cabs often have automatic mirror-adjusting controls in the cab. Position the mirrors so that you can see everything behind you. Open the windows and physically turn your head to look through them before you set your wheels in motion, and while you're backing up.

Transmission. Some box trucks and stake- and flat-bed trucks have manual transmissions (see "I Can . . . Drive a Stick Shift!" page 156). The gearshift works like any other stick shift, except it is generally much more difficult or sticky to move. Make sure you feel very comfortable driving a stick before you rent, borrow, or buy a truck. Even if changing gears is a little challenging at first, as with any manual transmission vehicle, you will quickly learn the rhythm of your particular truck. Also, keep in mind that trucks have a much lower "speed ceiling" (the maximum speed at which you can comfortably and safely travel). For this reason, it's important to drive slowly and watch your speedometer carefully.

Clearance. Trucks tend to be much taller than cars, so you will need to be careful and make sure you can clear certain spaces. Many novice truck drivers make the mistake of entering into a parking garage or fast-food drive-through and get caught underneath the ceiling or awning. Know the height of the truck you are driving and, before entering any kind of enclosed space, like a tunnel, be sure to read the signs that indicate the clearance measurements.

Of course, once you've mastered these skills, you'll have to meander on down to your local truck stop and mosey up to the counter for a nice slice of pie. Before you know it, you'll be talking about your rig with the best of them!

GIRL'S WORLD

Monster truck rallies have long been a father-son bonding experience. Why not switch it up and bring your mom to this macho sporting event? Bring a couple of lawn chairs and a six-pack of your favorite beverage. You can people watch, learn all about the different trucks and engines, and make it a day to remember!

I Can... Fix a Bike Chain!

Fixing a bicycle chain is a simple skill that can be mastered in a matter of minutes. A woman who can fix her own bike chain is both impressive and independent. If you've never attempted to fix your own bike chain, follow this simple plan and get yourself back in the saddle again.

The Quick Fix

1. As soon as you feel that your chain has become jammed or has slipped off your bike, stop pedaling and dismount. Pull your bike off to the side of the road and move it to smooth space or clearing so that you have room to work and can see what you are doing.

2. Place the chain on the lower part of the smallest front chain ring and align it on the wheel's sprocket.

3. Pull the chain above and away from the chain ring with one hand while using the other hand to rotate the pedals back-

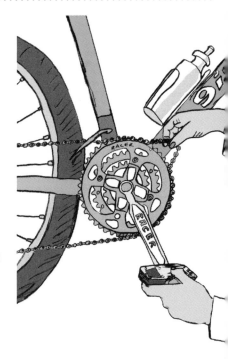

ward. The chain should fall into place and spin freely. If the chain gets stuck on a bolt on the chain ring, simply move the chain away from the bolt and place on the sprocket.

An Ounce of Prevention ··········

To make sure your bike chain does not come out of alignment easily you need to clean your chain regularly. For this job you'll need proper lubricating solvent and a clean cloth. Contrary to laymen's (pronounced "lame-men's") advice, gasoline and WD-40 should not be used, since they can damage the chain and keep it from functioning properly. Instead, use a lube designed for the bike chains (available at cycling stores). Follow this simple cleaning routine to maintain your chain and keep yourself from falling prey to the "chain of fools":

1. Prop your bike on a bike stand or lean it against a wall. Drip the lube onto the top of the chain and rotate the pedals backward.

The Jargon

Sprocket: A gear with metal teeth that mesh with a bike chain

Chain ring: The small and large rings that a move a bike chain

Drivetrain: The parts that make the back wheel spin and the bike move forward

Front or rear derailleur: The mechanism that pushes the chain from the chain ring at the front of the drivetrain

2. Once the chain has gone through one entire rotation around both the front chain ring and rear cogs, take the cloth and firmly rub the sides and top of the chain. Keep spinning the chain around with the pedals. Repeat the process until the cloth stops becoming black with grease.

3. Drip some of the lube onto a clean area of the cloth and rub the front chain ring and rear cogs clean, pinching the cloth around the top of the chain ring while you rotate the pedals backward. Clean both pulleys in the rear derailleur in the same manner.

4. Lightly drip the lube on the chain and rotate it around the chain rings. Hold up the rear of the bike and shift the gears so that the clean, lubed chain makes its way around all the gears.

Faking It!

Don't want to get your hands greasy from touching the chain? Hold the bike upright while standing to the side of the bike without the gears and chain ring. With your toe, step lightly onto the bottom of the loose chain and pull it slightly down and forward of the front chain rings. Move the chain onto the sprockets of the chain ring, remove your toe, and rotate the pedals backward so that the chain can fall into place. This technique takes a little practice, but it will allow you to keep your hands clean while looking incredibly cool and experienced.

I Can ... Pack a Car Trunk!

We never appreciated the gift of the "dad pack" until we had to do it ourselves. But making everything fit into a trunk is really just a simple exercise in space prioritizing.

To become an expert trunk packer, follow the easy steps below.

Key Techniques

1. Begin by examining the items you want to pack in the trunk. Mentally separate the hard objects from the soft items and organize them from largest to the smallest.

2. Start with any items that are large and rigid, such as boxes or suitcases. Place these items in the trunk on their widest, flattest side, with any handles or other protruding objects facing up or out. Be sure that you stack them as close to each other and as far to the back as you can.

3. Load the other large pieces into the trunk from largest to smallest, stacking and fitting them where appropriate.

4. Now you are ready to place your large, soft items in the trunk. Garment bags should be placed flat on top of suitcases for added protection.

5. Finally, sprinkle in any small soft items, such as purses. Pillows are a great way to cushion your load and fill in any gaps so that contents don't shift as you are driving. If possible, keep the items that you'll need soonest close to the opening of the trunk for easy access.

6. Be sure that you place any fragile items out of the way of trunk hinges and tuck them securely between soft objects that won't crush them during transport.

A well-packed trunk is a spectacle for all to behold. After putting these tips into practice, you too will marvel at how you managed to get all that stuff in there!

I Can... Ride a Motorcycle!

Let's face it: Less than 10 percent of motorcycle riders in this country are women. Why so few? Riding a motorcycle is definitely cool, chic, and sexy, but many women are intimidated by the idea of helming something that looks so macho and dangerous. But riding a motorcycle is an incredibly fun and liberating activity. Motorcycles are not just a hobby; they are a way of life. If you have ever been captured by the idea of hitting the open road on a bike, consider the easy tips below to help you get started on your adventure.

Get a Leg Up

If you can ride a bicycle and drive a stick shift, you have a better-than-average chance of succeeding on a motorcycle. And if you have excellent coordination between your hands and feet (which shift gears as well as work the clutch), you're in even better shape. If you have a friend with a motorcycle, ask to sit on it and get a guided tour of the gears and shifting mechanisms. You can learn a lot about the orientation of a bike without even starting the engine. This introduction will help you feel more comfortable when you begin your formal instruction.

Find Your Course

There are several national organizations, including the Motor Safety Foundation and the American Motorcycle Association, that offer two- and three-day motorcycle instruction classes. These classes fully immerse you in the world of the motorcycle, so you can expect to learn a great deal in a relatively short amount of time. By combining classroom instruction and road training, motorcycle classes like these give you a 360-degree view of life on a hog. Still, really learning to ride a motorcycle takes at least a year of additional practice.

Meet Your Maker

From Yamaha to BMW to Harley-Davidson, there are literally dozens of motorcycle manufacturers. The type of bike you choose depends on several variables: where you want to ride it, what type of riding you want to do on it, and what kind of image you want to project. If you are into cruising, you may want to check out a Harley. If showing off is your thing, a flashy Yamaha may be the one for you. If you like old-school design, a Ducati or vintage Indian Motorcycle (no longer made) might speak to you. Do your research and be sure to find a bike that fits your size. We recommend that you don't spend too much on your first bike, however, because you are

likely to fall in the beginning and cause some superficial damage to the body of the bike.

Wear Protection

Here comes the fun part—the clothes. What could be cooler than wearing a leather motorcycle jacket? But first things first. If you buy no other gear for yourself (and we're not recommending that), you must buy a helmet—a good one with ample padding. You don't want to become an organ donor before your time, do you?

Now that you've got yourself a helmet, go crazy and buy yourself a pair of leather pants (you actually have a legitimate reason to own them now!) and tall motorcycle boots. Conveniently, motorcycle boots add several inches of height (great for short women) and, of course, protection from nasty scrapes should you fall.

The Open Road

After you have successfully completed your training, you will need to take a road test at the DMV. Passing this test will make you an official, licensed biker. With your motorcycle license in your back pocket, get out there and hit the open road. In your first year, build your confidence by getting out to the country as often as possible and practicing your skills at low speeds. As you gain more experience you can take to the highway, knowing you have the skills to make it on more hectic terrain.

EXTRA CREDIT!

Motorcycle rallies bring together bikers from all over the country and are a great way to meet other motorcycle enthusiasts. Select the right rally for you based on the location, time of year, or even type of bike you own.

Are You a Gear Hero or a Zero?

1. A sprocket is

   a. A gear with metal teeth that mesh with a bike chain

   b. A type of wrench

   c. A *Star Trek* character

2. One of the best knots to use to strap something to a car is

   a. The bowline

   b. The granny

   c. The nuptial

3. Practice parallel parking between

   a. Two traffic cones

   b. Two parked cars

   c. Two traffic cops

4. The best place for a suitcase is

   a. The trunk

   b. The right side of the backseat

   c. The top of the car, fastened with bungee cords

5. When driving a truck it is essential to use

   a. Your mirrors

   b. Your horn

   c. Your intuition

Mostly *A*'s: Formula One!

You are a true gearhead and will never be intimidated by that strange squeaking noise coming from your car ever again!

Mostly *B*'s: Sunday Driver!

You mean well but you sometimes get your wires crossed. What you lack in skill you make up for in enthusiasm, but don't blame us when you blow up your engine.

Mostly *C*'s: Student driver!

You need to go back to Driver's Ed. immediately! You are a menace on the roads and are about as useful to a car as an empty gas tank!

Nature Calls

Scientists can tell us that the whole notion that women belong indoors and men belong out dates to Neanderthal times, when the cavemen went out to hunt and forage for food and left the women at the pad to take care of the kiddies and tend the fire. Theoretically, this was because women weren't strong enough to do the hunting and gathering. But we can't help wondering if the men were simply keeping the fun stuff for themselves!

It's now the twenty-first century, and times and roles have changed. After a long day tackling all of the challenges we women face indoors (school work, office work, caring for the kids, washing the dishes, paying the bills), we could use some serious therapy from Mother Nature. Next time you're stressed out, imagine getting together with a group of girlfriends and heading out into the wilderness. With the skills you learn in this chapter, you will be able to fend for yourself and have a blast while you're at it! Whether you're firing up the barbecue or skipping a stone across a placid lake, you will relish the freedom the great outdoors has to offer.

As you fall asleep under the stars, you just might fantasize about a future in which we women can hunt and gather with the best of them. A future in which we can row our boat upstream, clean our own fresh-caught dinner, build the fire to cook it on, and then sit around spitting while the men do the dishes.

I Can . . . Barbecue!

Before the advent of professional-grade convection ovens and stainless-steel gas grills, grilling had to be done over an open fire. While the technology has certainly advanced, there is still something delectable about that old-fashioned, char-grilled flavor. If you are a queen in the kitchen, there's nothing stopping you from walking those skills outside and cooking over an open flame under the open sky.

It's a Grill Thing

When choosing a grill, deciding between gas and charcoal is a matter of preference. Learn your grill preferences by asking friends and relatives which method they use—and sampling their food, of course! While gas grills are certainly easier to clean and maintain, many grill connoisseurs say that when it comes to taste, nothing beats an old-fashioned charcoal grill. Here's the chill way to grill:

1. Stack the coals, using the traditional pyramid method. Begin by placing fifteen to twenty coals in a single layer on the lower cooking grate. Continue to layer and stack additional coals in a pyramid shape. The top coal should almost touch your top grill grate. Squirt lighter fluid sparingly over the coals, using slightly more on the center of the pyramid.

2. Light your coals using a flame starter with a long handle, or long matches.

Small matches are dangerous. In a pinch, you can use a taper candle to light your grill, but just be sure a lot of wax does not drip on the coals—this could hamper the flame.

3. Once lit, coals are generally ready in about fifteen to twenty minutes. You can speed the process by adjusting the vents on the kettle of your grill to allow adequate air circulation. You'll know they are ready when the coals are white just at their edges. Now you're ready to put your meat (or vegetables) on the barbecue and start cooking.

Perfect Cooking Times · · · · · · · · · · ·

While cooking times vary based on the thickness and cut of your meat, here are some general guidelines:

Beef: 6 to 8 minutes per side (more if you like your meat well done)

Chicken and pork: 5 to 6 minutes per side

Fish: 1 to 3 minutes per side

Hot Tips for Grilling · · · · · · · · · · · · · ·

Don't let those loudmouth grillers fool you—mastering the grill is as simple as putting on your apron, rolling up your sleeves, and following a few simple rules:

• Invest in a set of grill tools. Do not use common kitchen utensils such as tongs or forks to tend to the barbecue. Doing so will damage the items and might even result in injury.

• Always make sure there is enough food to go around. Because grilled food is a treat, people tend to eat more than they would normally. Prepare for this and grill twice as much food as you would usually need.

• Marinate your meat and vegetables for at least an hour before you grill to let the maximum flavor sink in.

• Fish tends to fall apart and may slip through the grate when cooked, so use a cool tool called a grill back or place the fish on foil before grilling.

- Never apply oil or cooking spray to your grate after you've lit the coals. If you need to oil your cooking grate, do so before you light any fires.

- Watch for flare-ups, which result from too much fat mixed with too much heat. To avoid flare-ups, trim excess fat off of meat so that it does not drip onto the flames below.

- Don't forget to wear a tall white chef's hat and "Kiss the Cook" apron for added attention.

I Can... Clean a Fish!

You've cooked breaded fish sticks, prepared halibut fillets, and marinated salmon steaks, but have you ever had the satisfaction of catching your own dinner? Of course not, because then you would have had to clean it. Let the scales fall from your eyes— cleaning a fish is actually easy, fun, and not terribly gross. All you need is a cutting board, sharp knife, and these instructions.

Key Techniques

1. Cleaning a fish can be messy, so start by covering your work space with paper grocery bags or newspaper. You'll also want to have a plastic bag handy for the guts and bones that you will be pulling from the fish.

2. Place your fish in a colander under a faucet or other water source and run water over the body until it is free of any slime. Using a sharp knife, cut off the fins on both sides of the fish. If your fish has scales, use a sharp knife tilted at a 90-degree angle to shear them off from end to head. Continue scraping until the body is smooth.

3. Insert the blade of your knife into the vent, the small opening near the tail of the fish. Slice lengthwise through the belly all the way up to the gills. Using a spoon, scoop out the guts from the cavity until you can see the spine of the fish.

4. Unless you're planning to cook the fish whole, cut the head off with your knife, making sure not to lose too much meat.

5. Cut along the top, or dorsal, fin of the fish. Pop out the dorsal fin by pulling on the spine from tail to end as if unzipping a zipper. This step will ensure that your guests will not have to pick out small bones throughout their meal.

GIRL'S WORLD

Gather a group of your most fun and adventurous women friends and plan a girls' fishing trip. Imagine the fun you will have together hanging out on a boat moored on a serene lake, kicking back with your pals while sipping on a beer. You'll have such a good time that you won't even mind cleaning fish!

I Can... Have a Sense of Direction!

For those of us without a sense of direction, it's difficult to conceive of the fact that "orienteering"—that is, getting lost on purpose in order to find the way back—is actually a hobby for thousands of people. This is one club we'll never join. Still, we yearn to be able to find our way without relying on help from the local 7-Eleven clerk. The ability to get one's bearings and follow a map is critical to being an independent and savvy traveler. And we can do it!

Orient Yourself

Finding north is key to developing a good sense of direction. To figure out where you are in relation to the direction north, follow these simple steps:

1. During the daytime you can find north by first finding east. Just locate the direction where the sun rose that morning.

2. Facing east, simply turn your body 90 degrees to the left. You are now facing north. From here, west is to your left, east is to your right, and south is, obviously, behind you. Keep this positioning in mind as you travel.

Study the Map

You may vaguely remember how to read a map from your seventh-grade geography class. Just in case you've forgotten, we'll refresh your memory now.

Take a look at a map. See the legend in a little box, probably near the bottom? All maps include legends that explain the symbols found on that map. Study the legend and figure out the scale you are working with. Use your finger to measure the distance and help you plot your route. Note the differences between interstate highways, freeways, and primary and secondary highways. If you are studying a trail map, be sure to look for changes in elevation that will affect your journey.

EXTRA CREDIT!

Close your eyes and plop your finger down on a spot on a map of your state. Take a road trip to this location, using only your brain and your map to guide you there. Do not cheat by getting directions online or from a friend. You will feel a great sense of satisfaction when you take a journey without needing anyone's sense of direction but your own.

Imagine Yourself from Above · · · ·

Whether you are out in the woods or walking the city streets, try to visualize yourself and your surroundings from above. In doing this, you will begin to get a better mental picture of your actual location relative to the map. Experts say that moving back and forth between a map and real-life orienting helps you internalize a stronger sense of direction.

I Can... Build a Fire!

They say that one of the first major steps in human progress was the moment humans discovered fire. You can get a taste of this primal thrill by learning how to build a fire yourself! The kind of fire you choose to build depends largely on your environment and the kind of wood and/or materials available to you. We'll focus on the basic campfire, showing you how to light a fire that will burn strong and last for hours.

Making Preparations

Of course, when you're camping you should carry matches and lighters in waterproof bags. But if these somehow end up getting soaked, you can always turn to your handy flint-and-steel set (found at most outdoor gear stores), which will work even when wet. To use it, first find some dry wood shavings, paper, or grass to use as tinder and keep them close by. Then hold the steel striker (the curved band of steel) in one hand and the flint stone in the other. Hold the curved blade steady and strike the stone downward against it. Repeat until you see a spark, and then quickly grab your tinder to catch the spark and start your flame burning.

Building the Fire

Begin by gathering a mixture of dry wood and kindling. You can use a combination of split wood (if available) or logs and smaller twigs and branches. If you are in a wet area, look for dead branches on trees rather than branches on the ground. It's very easy to underestimate your firewood needs, so collect about twice as much wood as you think you will actually use.

Next, you'll arrange your wood in the shape of an upside-down cone or tepee. Start by propping the larger branches up against each other, and then insert the smaller sticks in between the larger ones. Tuck the smallest pieces inside the tepee at the center. You can also put crumpled newspaper or other paper, if available, at the base of the tepee to help ignite the fire. Using a match, lighter, or tinder, light the small twigs or newspaper. If the fire does not immediately catch, gently fan it to increase the oxygen getting to the flame and encourage it to grow.

As the fire burns, the outside logs will fall toward the center and continue to feed the fire (you can poke the logs inward with a branch if you need to). Built using this technique, the fire will naturally burn itself out. If you are worried about the fire getting out of hand after you go to sleep, you can dump dirt or sand on the campfire to help snuff it out before you crawl into your sleeping bag. That being said, never bury a fire—the embers stay hot for a long time, and an unsuspecting person might get a nasty burn if he were to tread on them.

Faking It!

If you find yourself needing to start a fire without matches or a lighter, use a lens from a camera, telescope, or binoculars instead. Angle the lens so it reflects the sun directly onto the tinder. When the tinder starts to smolder, fan and blow gently until it ignites. The downside? This method only works during the day—and sunny days at that.

I Can... Row a Boat!

"Row, row, row your boat gently down the stream." The traditional nursery song makes it sound so easy. The truth is that rowing a boat takes a little bit of skill and a whole lot of practice. If you have not had the pleasure of rowing a boat by yourself or with a friend, we highly recommend the experience. The act of moving through the water is soothing and therapeutic. To fully enjoy the experience, you'll need to follow the basic steps below.

Key Techniques

1. Climb into the middle of the boat carefully, evenly balancing your weight in the boat so you don't tip over, and take your seat. If you are going to be rowing with a friend, coordinate your entries so that you both don't end up in the drink.

2. Situate yourself comfortably between the oars. Grip the handle of each oar. Your forearms should be angled so your wrists and elbows drop slightly below your hands. The blades of the oars should be in the water, at right angles to the surface.

3. Begin your stroke by leaning forward, hinging at the hips, with your arms straight. Now bend your arms and pull the oars back. You should lean back and straighten your legs as you pull. Your posture is key to your strength, so be sure to sit up tall and straight.

4. Extend your arms out in front of you, leaning forward again, and slowly dip the

oars back into the water—always keeping them at right angles to the water—and repeat. Remember, at the end of each stroke, allow your blades to emerge out of the water before you lean forward, move the tips of the oars back to the starting position, and dip them back into the water.

5. When you are ready to change direction, you can use one of your oars to pivot. Drag the right oar in the water to move left, and vice versa.

Okay, we admit that spitting is a gross habit and a public nuisance. Still, haven't you always wondered just exactly how guys manage to project their saliva over distances of 10 to 15 feet? It's gross, but fascinating.

Spit It Out

The trick to achieving a great spit is to first build up saliva in your mouth. The best way to do this is to pop in a mouth-watering candy like a sour gummy chew. Once you have obtained an adequate amount of saliva in your mouth, you are ready to practice spitting.

Find a place outside, preferably in a grassy and remote location where no one will be subjected to your unsavory practice. Without swallowing, draw the saliva down into the back of your throat, creating momentum. Imagine yourself to be like a pitcher winding up to throw a baseball, or a pinball player pulling the knob back before letting the ball fly.

To launch your saliva as far as possible you need to project it from a place of power. Many expert spitters say that they actually engage their abdominal muscles in order to help their spit catch air.

The final power move happens in your mouth, using your tongue, teeth, and roof of your mouth. You can practice the send-off by repeating the word "fooey." This exercise will help you propel your spit as if you were launching a rocket.

Disgusted yet? Fine. But when you have some time on your hands, some chewy candy in your purse or pocket, and no one around to say "Eeew," give your saliva a whirl. With enough practice, you'll be able to break the distance record next time you play with the boys.

I Can... Skip a Stone!

We were always in awe of our older boy cousins who, with the flip of a wrist, could send a flat rock bounding across the surface of the lake. It looked so magical and so . . . cool. Our attempts to skip stones usually resulted in a paltry but hopeful jump followed by a rapid plop into the water. What was that magical trick those boys seemed to have up their sleeves? Turns out it wasn't magic, but a good dose of science.

Key Techniques

1. Choose the right stone. A good skipping stone is wide and flat—almost the size of your palm, and uniform in thickness. It should also be a comfortable throwing weight, the approximate heft of a tennis ball. If your stone is too heavy, it won't be aerodynamic. If it is too light, it won't pick up enough velocity to skip.

2. Hold the stone between your thumb and middle finger, with your thumb on top and your index finger curved along the edge.

3. Stand at a slight angle facing the water. Hold this position as you carry through your throw. Your wrist should be fully cocked, as if you were pitching a baseball, when you release the stone. Remember to keep your hand low and your eyes on the surface of the water.

4. Before you toss the stone, picture yourself throwing out and down at the same time, launching the stone almost parallel to the water, as if you were trying shave the surface. You'll want to try

throwing as fast (but not as hard) as you can, because swiftness is the key. Now, release the stone, using the classic sharp wrist snap in order to put some spin on it.

5. Bask in the tranquil moment as you watch your stone dance across the water.

Random Fact: The record for stone skipping is held by a Texas man, who managed an impressive thirty-eight skips with one throw!

I Can . . . *Chop Wood!*

You can't be a "rugged individualist" if you lack the ability to chop your own firewood. If you've never done it before, the idea of chopping and splitting wood might sound intimidating, but lumber-Janes tell us that swinging an ax is quite exhilarating. So grab a log and put on your flannel shirt. After this short lesson, you too can experience the thrill of a hearty chop!

An Ax to Grind

Axes come in an array of shapes and sizes. There are axes with single bits (one sharp side) and double bits (two sharp sides). Axes with single bits are the safest and easiest for beginners to use. We recommend starting out with a "scout ax," a smaller version of a typical single-bit ax. As you improve your chopping skills, you may move up to a larger ax.

If you're going to chop with a used ax, make sure the blade has recently been sharpened. A dull blade is dangerous because it will splinter the wood, causing chips to fly at you.

How to Chop

Chopping down a tree usually requires a chainsaw and is very dangerous, so let's assume your tree has already been felled (cut) for you. As a beginner, you should select a soft wood such as pine or spruce on which to hone your skills.

The key to safe and proper ax use is your grip on the ax. If you are right handed, place your left hand at the bottom of the ax and your right hand about two-thirds of the way up the handle. Make sure your hands are relatively clean and free of debris so that nothing comes between you and the ax you are holding. Now you're ready to start. Follow the directions below for safe and effective chopping:

1. Begin by placing your log on a solid flat surface such as a stump or the ground. Stand in front of the log with your shoulders relaxed, your feet about hip distance apart, and your hands holding the ax in the starting position described above. Before swinging your ax, visualize the following set of motions: With your hands gripped firmly in their starting position, carefully raise your ax over your right shoulder. With your lead hand on top, swing your ax down. Your right hand should slide gently down the handle toward your left as you are striking the wood.

2. Once you have visualized this motion, take a practice swing. Be sure to stay at a safe distance from the log to avoid injury from flying bits of wood or even the ax itself. When you are ready to take your first real swing remember to keep your arms straight as you lower down into your swing.

3. Remember, the force of your swing is not nearly as important as your accuracy. You should drive your ax into the wood at a 45-degree angle.

4. To chop a log into two pieces, adjust your swing to make a V-shaped cut in the wood. By cutting at an angle, you are following the grain of the wood and making it easier to cut through. Once you have cut a V shape out of the wood, you can begin to cut directly through the rest of the log.

Let's Split ·

Splitting wood is definitely much more advanced than chopping it. Unlike chopping wood, splitting a log is done with one fell swoop. The best way to learn is to watch a pro. We recommend calling a local firewood supplier to give you a lesson in splitting wood. Always wear safety goggles to avoid any eye injuries.

Stoppers, bends, hitches, and single loops. Parts of a roller coaster? Nope. These are actually some of the most common knot terms.

You could spend a lifetime, or at least a prison sentence, learning to tie all of the different types of knots there are. But knot crafting is not reserved for inmates, sailors, or boy scouts—knowing how to tie knots is a life skill that can help you out of a lot of jams. From securing something to a car to hoisting yourself to safety, tying a knot can be a lifesaver (literally). We've chosen four from the wide world of knots that we think will come in handy.

Basic Overhand Knot

This simple knot is useful in just about any situation.

1. If you are right handed, grab your rope in your left hand about a foot from the end.

2. With your right hand, make a loop, forming an *X* shape at the bottom of the loop where the rope crosses over itself.

3. Hold the *X* with your left hand while using your right hand to thread the end of the rope through the loop and give it a good pull.

Surgeon's Knot · · · · · · · · · · · · · · · · ·

Use this knot when you need to tie two lines together.

1. Lay your lengths of rope down, side by side, making sure that the ends overlap by about 6 inches.

2. Take both ropes together where they overlap and make an overhand knot, but don't pull the loop closed.

3. Pull the ends of both ropes through the loop again.

4. Tug both ends to pull the knot tight.

Bowline Knot ·

When you need to secure an item, this knot is the one to use.

1. Using nylon rope, make a small loop 18 to 24 inches from the end of the rope. This loop is called the "hole."

2. Bring the end of the rope up through the hole, around the rope, and back down into the hole.

3. Pull until the knot is tight.

Half Hitch ·

The half hitch is great for securing an item to a pole or post. To simplify our instructions, we'll refer to one side of the rope as A and the other side of the rope as B.

1. Using a single rope, loop it around the object you're trying to hitch to, from right to left. End B should be in your right hand and A in your left.

2. Loop it again from right to left so it's wrapped twice around the post or pole.

3. Side B should still be in your right hand and A in your left. Cross B below A, forming an X.

4. Insert the end of B through the hole formed at the top of the X. Again, B should end up in your right hand.

5. Next, wrap length B around length A, crossing first over the top, then underneath.

6. Finally, bring the end of A up through the loop formed and pull the knot tight.

Random Fact: Besides humans, there are two other types of animals that can tie knots. Gorillas have been observed tying knots in sapling branches in order to secure their bedding. Weaver birds can also tie dozens of different types of knots, using dried grass to build their beautiful and intricate nests.

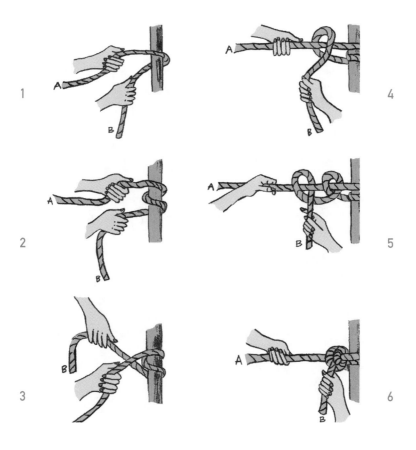

Half Hitch

Are You a Nature Bug or a Helpless Slug?

1. The fin on the top of a fish is called

   a. The dorsal fin

   b. The shark fin

   c. The flipper

2. Starboard and port are

   a. Directions on a boat

   b. A pair of crime-fighting sisters on a '70s TV show

   c. Two new brands of coffee-flavored liqueur

3. Which of the following will *not* help you produce more saliva and therefore spit further?

   a. Drinking water

   b. Thinking about a lemon

   c. Chewing a piece of soft candy

4. The angle that is most successful for skipping a stone is

   a. 20 degrees

   b. 30 degrees

   c. 90 degrees

5. Which of the following animals can tie a knot?

   a. A gorilla

   b. A panda bear

   c. A squirrel

Mostly *A*'s: Mountain woman!

The contestants on *Survivor* got nothing on you! You can wield an ax, clean your own dinner, and spit in the eye of any man who thinks his bowline is better than yours.

Mostly *B*'s: Girl Scout!

You can survive a hiking trip, but you aren't quite ready to really rough it. Limit your outdoor adventures to barbecuing and some gentle rowing.

Mostly *C*'s: City slicker!

Take our advice and never venture out of the city limits. Let's just say your survival skills are best suited to the *urban* jungle.

Afterword

So there you have it—everything you wanted to know (and a few things you probably didn't) about the not-so-mysterious world of men. And guess what—this stuff isn't just what they do; it's also what they talk about while they're doing it. As hard as it is to believe, if the man in your life says he played golf with Mike for four hours and all they talked about was football, scotch tasting, and what that burrito did to their stomachs (okay, we didn't cover absolutely *everything*), he is telling the complete truth. And to think they have been running the world all these years on that skill set!

We hope we have given you a starting point to get you in the game. We have covered a lot of topics—some practical and some not so practical—with an aim to demystify the stuff that the guys have been trying to keep to themselves. Now that you know how to join the office pool, swing an ax, and make a toast, a whole new world has opened up for you. However, be warned: Don't start ax wielding and picture hanging and tire changing too industriously. That would leave nothing for the guys to do. If you are putting up shelves, he should be cleaning windows, not reading *Playboy*. Our goal has been to give you the skills you need so you can choose the chores and activities you enjoy, not just the ones you've been taught.

Now get out there and start your old-girls' club, your girls-only poker night, and your women's tournament March Madness pool. But let's not let invite the boys. The fact that we now know how to do their stuff doesn't mean we actually want to hang out with them!

Acknowledgments

Leigh and Jennifer would like to thank all of the women they interviewed, especially Tricia Wright, Molly Sims, Kendra Danielsen, Sarah Noonan, Jen Rudd, Kate Scott, Tonya Phillips, and Erin Dayan. These women know how to slam a drink, fix a flat, tell a dirty joke, and even fire a shotgun. What more could anyone ask for?

Thanks also to Annie Barrows, Micaela Heekin, and Jay Schaefer.

Author Biographies

Leigh Phillips and Jennifer Axen are co-authors of *The Strippers Guide to Looking Great Naked*. Jennifer is a researcher and writer whose articles have appeared in publications from *Allure* to the *Onion*. She lives in Los Angeles. Leigh has a Master's degree in Women's Studies and Qualitative Research Methodologies from the University of Manchester (England) and lives in the San Francisco Bay Area.